LOVE, HONOR—and BE FREE

by
MAXINE HANCOCK

MOODY PRESS
CHICAGO

FOR

Margie Jones

Second Printing, 1975

ISBN: 0-8024-5021-0

The use of selected references from various versions of the Bible in this publication does not necessarily imply publisher endorsement of the versions in their entirety.

Printed in the United States of America

Contents

Acknowledgments

WHEN A HOUSEWIFE writes a book, she is her own cook and typist and researcher. But I have been greatly helped: by the patience of four little children—Geoffrey, Cammie-Lou, Heather Ruth, and Mitchell—and the encouragement and support of one forbearing husband, Campbell.

I am also grateful to the editors of *Moody Monthly* who granted me permission to use large portions of my article, "Career Wife to Housewife," published in that magazine in January 1971. It appears in this book as a substantial portion of chapter 17.

Not to be forgotten are all of the people who have shared their lives with me. They are in this book. The anecdotes are all true, but names and details are altered to protect their identities.

Above all, this is a book which could not have been written apart from God's enabling. It is a book which was given to Him in total and rededicated as each page was rolled into the typewriter. If there is any blessing in it, any help, any comfort—then all the thanks belong to Him.

Before We Start

The bold black-on-green posters were all over campus, announcing the next topic for the Debating Society:

RESOLVED: THAT WOMAN'S PLACE IS
BAREFOOT, PREGNANT & IN THE KITCHEN

I saw red then, and it still raises my blood pressure to hear discussion—especially by men—of "woman's place." Even Mother's Day sermons I find a bit hard to take. There's just *something* about hearing a man—any man—extol the virtues of dishwashing, nose-wiping, and floor-mopping, as though an annual pat on the back will keep us quiet and "in our place" for another year.

However, since those days that I spent on a poster-cluttered campus, I have spent a lot of time barefoot, pregnant, and in the kitchen. I married before completing my university degree, then studied side by side with my husband. After graduation, I spent a couple of years teaching high school English and then left the classroom to become a full-time housewife and mother. Because I am not the kind of woman who finds it easy to accept pat answers or to fill traditional roles just because they are traditional, I have done some hard thinking about the whole matter of being a woman in contemporary society.

9

In preadolescent days, I fumed about being a girl. "Boys have all the fun," I complained to my mother. And inwardly I rebelled, *I didn't ask to be a girl!* But never, since becoming one, have I wished to be anything but a woman. I like being a woman. I like nice clothes, swish hairdos, single long-stemmed roses in slender vases. I love to be loved. Bearing my children brought me moments of triumphant joy that nothing, I think, will ever match. Nurturing them is a challenge of the widest dimensions.

But I am not a particularly domestic sort of woman. I would rather read a book or write an article than sew or knit. I am too distracted to be a very good housekeeper. So, naturally, there have been dark days when I have thought, *A woman like me should never have married! I belong in a career—teaching in a university perhaps, reading erudite books—and here I am, hanging out diapers.* Since neither by temperament nor by natural talent or inclination am I the sort of woman who fits gracefully into the wife/mother pattern, I am just the sort of woman to whom women's lib philosophy is most attractive.

However, there is one other factor in the long equation by which I am working out, day to day, the solution to being a woman—a joyful, modern woman. And that factor is my relationship to the person of Jesus Christ. As a young girl, I responded in love and worship to Jesus Christ who, I understood, "suffered for sins, the just for the unjust, that he might bring us to God" (1 Peter 3:18). My faith in the Lord Jesus matured and deepened as it went through the tests of turbulent teenage doubts and rebellions, and later, frank and intellectual questioning. Through it all, Jesus Christ came through as being real, and personal, and God. I live my life in discipleship to Him.

And because of this discipleship to the Lord Jesus Christ, I come to some far different conclusions regarding my personhood and my womanhood from those being loudly

10

voiced by spokeswomen today. In obedience to Him, I turn to the Scriptures to find God's revealed truth. What I find in the Bible often goes against the grain of my naturally stubborn and independent disposition. Yet it has been my experience in every sector of my life, that the more closely I conform to the teachings of the Word of God, the happier, freer, and more fulfilled I am. I am convinced that the guidelines of the Bible with regard to womanhood (and with regard to everything else, for that matter) cannot be dismissed as the product of long-past cultures with built-in biases and inequalities. Rather, I see them as transcending human culture, based on God's total knowledge of woman, and designed to give her the fullest and happiest life possible.

The Christian woman does not look at the world as centering in the big letter "I." She knows that serving herself can bring only disappointment and frustration to herself, and damage to others. She knows that any emancipation which frees her only to serve her own self-interests is just another kind of servitude. Neither, on the other hand, does the Christian woman look at a world with a man at the center. No matter how dearly she loves that man, she knows that life centered in him will ultimately leave her unsatisfied.

The Christian woman, equally with the Christian man, has a world view and a life view which center in Christ. And thus, she sees things differently from either the radical liberationist or the woman for whom life is made up of husband, home, and children. The Christian's life goal can never be merely to please or "fulfill" herself. Nor can it be merely to please her husband or family. Hers is a bigger, more exciting goal: to please Him who has "called [her] with an holy calling" (2 Timothy 1:9) to minister with her gifts and abilities so "that God in all things may be glorified" (1 Peter 4:11). The Word of God tells her how to achieve this. Finding out what it tells her, and how to go

11

about implementing these instructions in her daily life: these are the challenging tasks of Christian womanhood.

In this book, I want to share with you some of the things that I have learned from my own study in the Scriptures, from observing others in their success and failure, and from the daily experience of hammering out an acceptance of my roles. I am certainly not an expert. I have not arrived. I am just another young woman caught in the ferment of ideas, the onslaught of the media on long-held values, and the day-to-day crunch of family living. My children are still very young (from three to eight years old). My husband is deeply involved in a developing business. As a Christian woman, I work daily to adjust the demands of my family, my community, my church, and myself, under the overriding demands of my Lord and Saviour Jesus Christ.

I don't expect that you will accept all my conclusions. But if you will grant the relevance and reliability of the Bible, I do not think we will differ widely on basic principles. And from that point, you will be able to work toward your own stance as a Christian woman in a changing society.

Part 1

MARRY–and Be Free

1

Mutual Submission

I GO BAREFOOT whenever I can. I like bare feet on clean floors and warm garden soil and cool, prickly grass. I like to feel with my feet. But I would not take very kindly to anyone suggesting that I *ought* to be barefoot—because, of course, I also like wearing shoes.

"Barefoot." The word has become a sort of hieroglyph—a simple word picture—for the effect on woman of the dominant male, forcefully keeping woman "in her place," wielding the power of his dollars over her total life. It is a word that is loaded with connotation: humility, servitude, dependency, poverty. And such connotations are most repugnant to the modern woman. Even to one like me who enjoys going barefoot.

Really, the word brings into focus the whole business of how males and females relate to each other, especially in that closest of relationships: marriage. Are women supposed to be subservient? How can we reconcile such a phrase as the apostle Paul's notorious "Neither was the man created for the woman; but the woman for the man" (1 Corinthians 11:9), with the strong-minded, clear-headed, well-educated womanhood of today?

There are many who feel that such reconciliation is impossible. Monica was one of them. Fresh from conscious-

15

ness-raising sessions, she was discussing women's rights with me.

"I'm just as keen as you are for 'full identity,'" I said, in the course of our conversation. "But I still come face to face with the scriptural principle that wives are to submit to their husbands."

"That's Paul," Monica interrupted. "I can't accept Paul on the subject. He's warped."

"Well," I tried again, "I accept Scripture as revelation, and on that basis I take Paul seriously on any count."

"Even when he says wives should submit to their husbands?" she asked, disbelieving that anyone could be so docile.

"Even then," I said.

"Why doesn't he also say for husbands to submit themselves to their wives?" she rasped.

"He does!" I said.

Monica's jaw dropped in surprise. She had missed, as most people do, that the passage in Ephesians which deals with the relationship of wives and husbands is set in a context summed up by the phrase, "Submitting yourselves one to another" (Ephesians 5:21).

In fact, this passage sets out not just one principle of marital relationship, but three:

Principle 1. Mutual Submission: ". . . submitting yourselves one to another in the fear of God" (Ephesians 5:21).

Principle 2. Voluntary Submission: "Wives, submit yourselves unto your own husbands, as unto the Lord" (Ephesians 5:22).

Principle 3. Love: "Husbands, love your wives, even as Christ also loved the church, and gave Himself for it" (Ephesians 5:25).

16

I think that these three interlocking principles are the basic building blocks of a sound and strong Christian marriage. Let's look at them one at a time.[1]

PRINCIPLE 1: MUTUAL SUBMISSION

The idea of mutual submission is at the very heart of any relationship between two people who share a common allegiance to Jesus Christ. It is a revolutionary concept which the Lord Jesus introduced to His disciples. He told them about it: "Ye know that . . . the Gentiles exercise dominion. . . . But it shall not be so among you," He insisted. "Whosoever will be chief among you, let him be your servant" (Matthew 20:27). He Himself demonstrated this principle, most memorably at the Last Supper when He got up from the table to perform the slave function of foot-washing. "If I then, your Lord and Master, have washed your feet; ye also ought to wash one another's feet," He explained (John 13:14). I suppose if the Last Supper were to have been held in contemporary society, Jesus would have done the dishes.

Competing for power is ruled out for Jesus' disciples. Of course, this principle applies first to relationships of all believers within the church. "Let nothing be done through strife or vainglory; but in lowliness of mind let each esteem other better than themselves," Paul admonishes the Philippians (2:3) and points out the self-emptying example of Christ Jesus who "took upon him the form of a servant" 2:7).

As Jonathan Edwards pointed out, the home is "the little church." And competition for power within the home structure is totally foreign to a Christian view which places the highest value not on power, but on service. So it is that

[1] Principle 2 begins in chap. 2; principle 3 is discussed in chap. 5.

17

when Paul urges the Ephesians to submit themselves to each other, the basis of his appeal is "the fear of Christ" (NASB[2])—reverence for, and obedience to our Lord.

Clearly then, in a marriage between two Christians, there is to be mutual submission. This is inherent in the idea of each partner attempting to please and make the other one happy. And it will be based on deep and sure mutual respect. A man who marries a woman whom he considers to be a birdbrain is unlikely to submit to her in anything; the woman who marries a man whose judgment she does not respect will find submission to that man very difficult. But when marriage is based on mutual respect, each partner will be submissive to the other.

This concept of mutual submission is underlined in Paul's practical and considerate instructions concerning sex in marriage: "The man should give his wife all that is her right as a married woman, and the wife should do the same for her husband: for a girl who marries no longer has full right to her own body, for her husband then has his rights to it, too; and in the same way the husband no longer has full right to his own body, for it belongs also to his wife. So do not refuse these rights to each other" (1 Corinthians 7:3-5, TLB[3]).

And the principle of mutual submission is exemplified by couples in Scripture. Abraham and Sarah, for one. It is this marriage to which Peter points as an example of classic wifely submissiveness (in 1 Peter 3:6). Yet a close look at the record shows that while Sarah did submit to Abraham, she nonetheless was quite capable of taking initiatives within the marriage. Not all of her suggestions were good ones —but then neither were all of Abraham's above reproach. One case is of special interest: Sarah felt strongly that Hagar and her mocking son must be expelled. And God Himself

2 New American Standard Bible

18

concurred with her, saying to Abraham, "in all that Sarah hath said unto thee, hearken unto her voice" (Genesis 21:12).

Mutual submission is a principle upon which individual competencies can be recognized—regardless of which partner has the expertise. I think of a young man who was embarking on a life in the ministry. He was determined that his home would follow the scriptural principle of wifely submission, but missed out on the prior principle of mutual submission. Although his wife was an intelligent and gifted woman, he gave her no opportunity to exercise a ministry— even to him. He was impoverished in his own life and teaching accordingly. Another young man, also married to an intelligent and original woman, invites her assistance as he prepares and studies. And so, in mutual submission, the streams of two lives converge into a wider, more powerful outflow.

Mutual submission, based as it is on reverence for Christ and respect for each other, is fed by little courtesies. Early in marriage, patterns of voice and tone are established.

We all know some pairs who seem to specialize in public put downs of each other. "Roger's such a dumb-dumb!" Rhoda says disparagingly—and tells a story to prove it. Roger is unable to defend himself without looking like even more of a dumb-dumb, so he retaliates by sharing Rhoda's most recent housekeeping or cooking failure. Other couples are not quite so open but make small, snide digs at each other for the amusement of the group. The fact is that few people are amused. Most feel both embarrassed and tense to be required to witness the sparring. No matter how lightly derisive things are said to or about each other, the couple which indulges in this habit erodes away the very foundation of their marriage. They undermine mutual respect.

[3] *The Living Bible*

The couple who speak warmly and proudly of each other may not be so funny at a party. But they are building and buttressing that mutual respect which is basic to mutual submission.

Jesus' principle of strength through meekness is still very little understood. It is often hard to apply in our everyman/woman-for-himself society. But it is the key to relationships which deepen and develop in joy. Any home which is a battleground for the sexes is clearly an unhappy and tense atmosphere—and surely not a home which can properly be termed "Christian."

However, having said this about the first great scriptural principle governing interpersonal relationships, we must still reach out and grasp that thorny passage: "Wives, submit yourselves unto your own husbands." This is said as a special and definitive application of the principle of mutual submission which we have discussed. Generally speaking, Paul says, all Christians should submit to each other. In particular, he goes on, wives should submit to their husbands. Why? Is this an outdated principle? Or is it still a valid basis for satisfying male-female relationships?

2

Voluntary Submission

THE FELLOW who sat next to Cam in Ethics 397 was a friend of mine from high school days. He didn't hide his interest in meeting my husband. Just what sort of man had Maxine married? And what sort of guy had felt he could live with Maxine for a lifetime? In high school days, I had been president, editor, secretary, or chairman of a long list of student activities. So when my old classmate met my new husband, he was decidedly curious. One day when he felt he knew Cam well enough to ask, he ventured, "I hope you don't mind me asking—but, well, just who is boss in your house, anyway?"

Cam and I had a good chuckle about the question—and the curiosity behind it. But the question was certainly not entirely a joke. Perhaps no one wondered any more than I did myself just how a dominant, strong-willed woman like myself would fit into my role as a marriage partner. Probably no woman has chafed any more against the repeated New Testament injunction "Wives, submit" than I have.

But the early years of our marriage were in no way the private version of *The Taming of the Shrew* they might easily have been. The Lord gave me a man just as strong-minded and strong-willed as I was myself. A man who occasionally could—and did—say, "Sit down, shut up, and listen here!

21

You're not the only one with an idea in your head." And the Lord also gave me guidelines, visible in the best marriages that I observed and clearly stated in the Bible. So in those first years of marriage, I began to learn to respect—and live— the pattern set out in Scripture for male-female relationships within marriage—the pattern which is stated succinctly in the phrase, "Wives, submit." And that brings us to the second great principle.

PRINCIPLE 2: VOLUNTARY SUBMISSION

Even before marriage, I was convinced that there was no way to evade what Scripture had to say about the order of things within the home. I had enough experience with obeying—and disobeying—God's commands in other areas of my life to know with surety that disobedience in my life would certainly result in unhappiness, that obedience and discipleship would result in joy. And since I wanted to build the best possible marriage as the framework for the happiest possible home, soon after marriage I hit the Book in an attempt to come to grips with an overall concept of male-female relationships—from God's point of view.

From this study came several insights which have helped me greatly in my adjustments to being a woman in accordance with God's patterns.

First of all, it became abundantly clear from a study of the New Testament that the browbeaten (barefoot!) wife was just as foreign to the thinking of the inspired writers as was the henpecked husband. Both are wide deviations from God's norms. There is no injunction anywhere in Scripture which tells husbands to "rule your wives." Always, the command is to the wives: "Wives, submit."

Now this opens up a prospect to me which is far more inviting than that of being "put in my place." Given to me is the opportunity of accepting a position—not as a sign of subservience or an acquiescence to inferior status—but as a voluntary, rational acceptance that God has made an order which is for the good of men and women alike and which, followed, will produce the greatest human happiness.

Once I really understood that submission was up to me to accept—not up to my husband to impose—my response to the idea of submission changed. And I wonder how many women there are who are daring their husbands to put them in their place, defying them even, who would stop such foolishness if they realized that true submission is not something which God intended should be imposed upon them, but rather something which they would enter into voluntarily, intellectually, and in obedience to the Lord Jesus Christ.

In this approach to submission, the woman finds herself being "conformed to the image of his Son" (Romans 8:29). For in our Lord we know One who, though in all respects fully equal with God, was able to give the Gethsemane cry, "Nevertheless not my will, but thine, be done" (Luke 22:42). That's the ultimate submission.

And the end result of Christ's submission was the fulfillment of God's will. This, too, is the result of a woman's willing and voluntary submission to her husband. In Christ's case, His submission brought salvation for the whole world. In the wife's case, her submission can bring salvation to her whole household (1 Peter 3:1-2; 1 Corinthians 7:14).

Just as Jesus' submission ultimately led to His glorification (Philippians 2:9), so too the submissive woman eventually finds that in submission she has found real glory: "Her children arise up, and call her blessed; her husband also, and he praiseth her. . . . Favour is deceitful, and beauty is vain: but a woman that feareth the LORD, she shall be praised" (Proverbs 31:28-30).

So I came to accept the principle of submission. But in the back of my mind still lurked the nagging question: Why me? Why should the woman take the role of submission?

Why did God choose us to be the ones to identify with Christ in this particular way?

And to grapple with that question, I turned back to the creation accounts, to discover the background to this God-ordained relationship between man and woman.

First of all, I found that "God created man in his own image, . . . male and female created he them" (Genesis 1:27). What a beautiful sentence that is! And surely it deserves at least equal time with some of the deductions which have been drawn from the creation story. God made man—male and female—in His image. The Bible is not the basis for any concept of transcendent sex—that is, that God is male and creation female.[1] God is neither male nor female. And He gave each sex an equal share in His nature or "image." He commissioned them equally, too: "Be fruitful, and multiply, and replenish the earth, and subdue it" (Genesis 1:28). Both of the primary tasks given to mankind were tasks in which both sexes were to share. From the beginning, God intended they should be "heirs together of the grace of life" (1 Peter 3:7).

In chapter 2 of Genesis, a more detailed account of the creation of the human race is given. It is in this record that we learn of woman being made to meet man's need for a counterpart who could share life with him. No more than the first account, does this one suggest—or leave any room for thinking—that woman was thus in some way inferior to man. It is, indeed, exactly how large we write the letters M-A-N which will determine how large we write the letters W-O-M-A-N. For woman was made to correspond with man; she was to be—not as is often misquoted—an "help-mate," but rather "an help meet" (Genesis 2:18) for man.

---

[1] The view of sexuality as transcendent is explained in an article by Joan Lloyd, "Transcendant Sexuality as C. S. Lewis Saw It," *Christianity Today* 18, no. 3 (Nov. 9, 1973): 7ff.

That is, she is to be a helper suitable to his needs, complementary to his psychological makeup, equal with him in intellectual capacities.

That woman was created after man is certainly no indication of inferiority. As Ruth Schmidt puts it: "People who act as if the story of Eve's creation subsequent to Adam's makes woman less valuable should remember that if the ascending order of creation leads to the creation of man—it is *woman* who becomes the pinnacle of creation."[2] Nonetheless, she was, as Paul states, "made for man." But it is this same Paul who points out quickly, as an antidote to any misunderstanding, "For as the woman is of the man, even so is the man also by the woman; but all things of God" (1 Corinthians 11:12). So, as woman was originally made from man, all men thereafter drew their being from woman—and a true equality exists.

There are two really big concepts established in Genesis 2 which help us in our understanding of God's plan for male-female relationships. That the sexes were created equal is fully established. Equal, but different. Unisex is not God's idea. The sexes are distinct in far more than genital detail. Woman was created in a way which was complementary to man. Her lacks were his strengths; her strengths, his lacks. The sexual interlocking of bodies is only symbolic of the total psychological interlocking of personality which God intends in the relationship of marriage—a relationship so complete in its knitting of two personalities that "they shall be one flesh" (Genesis 2:24).

Second, Adam was constituted the spiritual head of the union with Eve. God's design for male spiritual leadership was implicit in creation. Not only was Adam prior in creation; but, far more significant, it was Adam who re-

[2] Ruth Schmidt in a forum, "What Did Saint Paul Want?" *His* 33, no. 8 (May 1973): 13.

ceived God's word of prohibition regarding the fruit of the tree of the knowledge of good and evil. While, as we saw from Genesis 1, man and woman shared together in God's blessing and setting forth of tasks, we learn from Genesis 2 that Adam alone received the negative commandment and its accompanying warning: "In the day that thou eatest thereof thou shalt surely die" (Genesis 2:17).

The fact that God communicated His word to Adam places Eve in a position—not of inferiority of person—but of subordination of position. She learned this command from Adam, and was responsible to him first in obeying it.

Thus, from the very beginning, the "one flesh" which is produced through the union of man and woman had a definite structure ordained of God—a structure which prefigured that which would ultimately exist in "the body" which is the Church, produced through the union of believers with Christ. Paul's commentary validates this interpretation: "But I would have you know, that the head of every man is Christ; *and the head of the woman is the man*" (1 Corinthians 11:3).

God's plan, which installed man as the spiritual head of the woman in marriage, was not devised out of any "male chauvinism" on His part. But, just as later on His creative Spirit would provide the multimembered body of Christ with members having specific gifts and functions, so here, at the creation of man and woman, "there are diversities of gifts, but the same Spirit. And there are differences of administrations [ministries], but the same Lord. And there are diversities of operations, but it is the same God which worketh all in all" (1 Corinthians 12:4-6). In other words, in order that the home would be a healthy, well-functioning organism, God gave it a structure—"as it hath pleased him" (1 Corinthians 12:18). And that structure puts man at the head of the home.

His purpose in constituting the home—as well as the

26

church—is "that there should be no schism [division] in the body; but that the members should have the same care one for another" (1 Corinthians 12:25). No division in the body! A perfect union of persons. That ,is God's plan for male and female in marriage. It is one which is rarely fully realized. But understanding His design can go a long way in helping us fulfill it.

And that brings us to Genesis 3, the Fall. Genesis 1 stressed equality in creation. Genesis 2 stressed complementarity. And Genesis 3 shows how disobedience really messed up God's design.

Eve's part in the Fall is kind of hard for women to accept. Did Satan come to her because she was the "weaker sex"? I don't think so. I think that Eve was vulnerable to Satan's subtle temptation just because she was in a position of subordination to her husband. And, while not phrased that way, Satan's temptation to her was to make a spiritual decision on her own, against the command of God expressed to her by her husband. Satan urged her to repeat his sin: that of rebellion against divine authority, the usurpation of authority by a subordinate. Thus, as Satan had said in his heart, "I will ascend into heaven, I will exalt my throne above the stars of God ... I will be like the most High" (Isaiah 14:13-14), so he invited Eve to rebel against the authority of her husband in order that together they could "be as gods" (Genesis 3:5).

Because of Eve's disobedience to Adam and thus, to God, sin entered the human race. And among the curses meted out to the offenders, God included this for Eve: "And thy desire shall be to thy husband and he shall rule over thee" (Genesis 3:16). Because Eve refused to accept the role of subordination voluntarily, she would now experience enforced subjection. This new subjugation would not be entirely because of the man's power hunger, but also because woman would have within herself a desire and psychological need to be ruled.

We know that in the Fall there were vast changes throughout creation. Many, many things were shifted or faulted out of their original alignments. This truth is brought home in Romans: "The whole creation groaneth and travaileth in pain together until now. And not only they, but . . . even we ourselves groan within ourselves, waiting for . . . the redemption of our body" (8:22-23). As I read Genesis 3 and compare it to my own observations of human nature, I can only feel that at the Fall there was a psychological faulting within woman. From that time on, she craved—actually desired—the mastery of a man who would rule over her.

Certainly, honest women would admit that the sort of man whom they most respect and admire is the man who is strong enough to express his will. And it has been obvious to me in a number of marriages that I have observed, that the most unhappy women are those who have been either unable to give in to, or in some cases, find at all, mastery in the men whom they have married. Let's face it: we have a desire for "husbanding"—for someone big enough and strong enough to be more than just a partner, someone to take the leadership of the home in every essential way.

"What about the cross?" someone is asking by now. "You're talking about the curse. Doesn't the cross end the curse? Isn't that what the death of Christ accomplished for us?" Before we can make the bold and attractive statement that the cross eradicates the curse, putting man and woman back on fully equal footing, we must examine rather carefully the effect of the cross on the curse in general.

Perhaps we can understand it best by analogy. Let's look at the effect of the cross on that ultimate curse—death. It is clear that Christ put death itself under a death sentence, that He abolished its ultimate power over human destiny.

28

And yet it is just as clear that today, as in Adam's day, human beings die physically before entering into eternal life. What exactly was the effect of Christ's death on death itself? Simply this: Jesus Christ, in His death and victorious resurrection, drew the sting from death:

> Oh death, where is thy sting? Oh grave, where is thy victory? The sting of death is sin, and the strength of sin is the law. But thanks be to God which giveth us the victory through our Lord Jesus Christ (1 Corinthians 15:55-57).

Christ's death, then, brought an amelioration of the death sentence. Death has lost its grip of terror (see Hebrews 2:15). For the believer, to die is to "sleep in Jesus" and so we "sorrow not even as others sorrow which have no hope" (1 Thessalonians 4:13-14). The cross means, too, that God has announced, "Death, thou shalt die!"[3] Death itself is under sentence in the final victory of Jesus Christ—that great day when the whole of creation will be redeemed, brought back into realignment with the purposes of its Creator.

Now, by analogy, it is not hard to understand just what Christ's death has accomplished for us as women. Of course He took the curse for us. Now "there is neither Jew nor Greek, there is neither bond nor free, there is neither male nor female: for ye are all one in Christ Jesus" (Galatians 3:28). Our standing before God is as equal as it was on creation day. But we are still living in a creation which is shifted out of line by the Fall, and our own natures are still touched by its effects. Like Eve, we desire husbands, want them. We cry out psychologically for their strength and

---

[3] John Donne, "Sonnet VIII," in *John Donne: Poetry and Prose* (Oxford: Clarendon, 1946), p. 65.

leadership. But in the New Testament pattern, the sting has been drawn from the rule of our husbands. For now, as Paul points out, the husband is to be Christlike in his love for the wife: self-effacing, self-giving. And for a woman who has learned the Christlike role of voluntary submission in order to carry out God's will, submission to a Christlike man, who is giving himself for and to her, is no very hard task. As Jesus said, "My yoke is easy, and my burden is light" (Matthew 11:30).

In fact, in the union of two obedient disciples of Jesus Christ—one male and one female—we get as close to the experience of Eden as we shall ever come. The result of voluntary submission of wife to husband is the joy and peace that comes from living in harmony with God's plan and with our own natures.

Eve in the garden was the first women's libber. Only through obedience to Christ can we be free from the heritage of heartbreak, friction, and competition which she handed down to us.

So—

> Wives, submit yourselves unto your own husbands, as unto the Lord. For the husband is the head of the wife, even as Christ is the head of the church: and he is the saviour of the body. Therefore as the church is subject unto Christ, so let the wives be to their own husbands in everything (Ephesians 5:22-24).

3

Areas of Submission

"OK," CATHY, a young married grad student, told me. "I'll accept that we are supposed to submit. But how? I mean, in what areas? Like, for instance, a lady in our discussion group said the other day, 'John doesn't like me to take the car out on icy days, so I missed that sale.'" Cathy laughed. "I just can't imagine that kind of submission."

"And I can't imagine that Art would ask you for that kind of submission," I concurred. "Areas of submission are highly individual and vary as much as the couple themselves and what it is they know about, and ask of, each other."

After my conversation with Cathy that day, I tried to work out in my own mind some of the practical details of submission. Just exactly what does it entail? And in what general areas is it applicable?

WHAT SUBMISSION IS NOT

Perhaps what submission *is* can be pointed out most clearly by stating some of the things which submission *is not.*

Submission is NOT denying selfhood. A woman is a person. Any woman who denies her own selfhood or "personhood" is in danger of becoming a thing instead of a person. The man you married loves you—as a person: a whole, total sum of traits and abilities. I cannot imagine the sort of man who would really prefer a deferential automaton to a clear-headed intelligent person who is a partner in every sense of the word, and who voluntarily submits to him.

Submission is NOT unquestioning acquiescence. Any decision is the better for two people's consideration. Ideas or judgments put forward by a man need the sharpening and clarifying—and even corrective—effect of thorough discussion. The woman who is most fully an "help, meet for him" is the one who evaluates her husband's views, weighs them, and discusses them with him. When she disagrees, there is no reason why she should not suggest possible alternatives. Submission is, ultimately, acquiescence. But it need not be silent, unquestioning, or unthinking.

Submission is NOT a tacit acceptance of inferiority. Acceptance of a subordinate position within the framework of marriage is not the same as accepting a sense of personal inferiority—as we have already pointed out in detail in our study of Genesis. Acceptance of personal inferiority leads to "doormatting." A woman who allows herself to become a convenient person for her husband to belittle is underestimating both herself and the need of her husband for a strong and resilient partnership in marriage. Submission should be made in an attitude of personal dignity and worth.

MAJOR AREAS

What, then, are some of the major areas in which submission is an operative principle within marriage? Recognizing how individual this is, I would venture to suggest three.

Submission in spiritual matters. As Adam was constituted the head of the first home in spiritual matters, so every married man is responsible to God for the spiritual guidance of his family. In our society there seems to be a prevailing tendency for women to be the spiritually strong mates. Where a man simply refuses to take his role as spiritual head, there is little for a woman to do except exercise some leadership herself. However, many men who sit back and let their wives take the lead would be capable of this leadership if the wives would be submissive to them and expect headship of them.

James H. Olthuis, in an article for the *Baker's Dictionary of Christian Ethics*, puts it this way:

> In marriage the husband is the head of the wife. . . . The husband is to take the lead in setting the religious direction of the marriage, its meaning, goals and purposes. Once the basic question is settled as to which vision of life is going to norm activities, who decides and leads in the day-to-day affairs of the marriage depends on the persons and situations involved.[1]

Submission in major decisions. Some of these decisions may include the husband's job or career, place of living, size of family, financial organization. Now, I am not suggesting that the husband would make a fiat in any or all of these areas. Any marriage which is based on anything but full and free discussion of ideas, with mutual respect and mutual submission, would be quite unsatisfactory.

However—and it is here that the administrative leadership of the husband comes into force—once there has been full and free discussion, thoroughly assessing the situation; once reasonable alternatives proposed by either mate have been properly considered; once varying areas of competency and expertise have been taken into account, then, ultimately— even if the wife remains in basic disagreement with her husband—pleasant acquiescence is her route.

It is this to which Peter refers when he speaks of believ-

[1] James H. Olthuis, "Marriage," in *Baker's Dictionary of Christian Ethics* (Washington, D.C.: Canon, 1973), p. 407.

ing women being "Sarah's daughters": "being in subjection unto their own husbands: even as Sarah obeyed Abraham, calling him lord: whose daughters ye are, as long as ye do well" (1 Peter 3:5-6). You will remember that obedience to Abraham must often have been against Sarah's better judgment. Once, for instance, she landed up in Pharaoh's court as a potential concubine (see Genesis 12:10-20). Nonetheless, she obeyed—unafraid because she trusted the Lord to work out His will in spite of her husband's mistakes.

Submission in the sexual relationship. A third area of submission is in sex within marriage. This is not to suggest that the wife should accept a role of passivity—something which has long since been repudiated by women. (And really, I wonder just how many Victorian wives really found sex as uninteresting as this century's critics would like to suppose. I like a line in Jessamyn West's *The Friendly Persuasion*: "Eliza [Quaker wife and mother] looked at the face that had always pleasured her."[2] I have a hunch that lots of husbands "pleasured" lots of wives long before sexual liberty was announced by the Kinsey report.)

Voluntary submissiveness in sex is far from passivity; it is, rather, an active desire to please and give pleasure to the other partner. An interesting finding in Maslow's psychological studies is cited in Friedan's *The Feminine Mystique*:

> The more "dominant" the woman, the greater her enjoyment of sexuality—and the greater her ability to "submit" in a psychological sense, to give herself freely in love.[3]

In pleasing her husband, a woman may well be sexually aggressive—often taking sexual initiatives—if that's what he

[2] Jessamyn West, *The Friendly Persuasion* (New York: Harcourt, Brace, 1940), p. 55.

[3] Betty Friedan, *The Feminine Mystique* (New York: Norton, 1963), p. 317.

34

likes. Paul, whom so many accuse of asperity with regard to marriage, is the writer who says, "Defraud not one another"—don't cheat each other of the sexual pleasures and privileges which marriage entitles you.

The wife who submits to her husband in bed will find other areas of marriage in which to submit to him—and find that they are just as productive of joy and harmony as is a good sexual relationship.

A BLEND

It is clear that most effective marriages work with a blend of mutual submission to each other and voluntary submission of the wife to the husband. A few years after Cam and I were married, Cam discovered that despite his challenging job as a school principal, his lifelong desire to farm was unabated. At first I was dismayed—to say the least. I was a city girl, and I had married a schoolteacher—not a farmer. It was my observation that farming, at best, provided a much more precarious existence than teaching. I tried to reason with him in this light.

Over the period of some months, however, I came to realize that Cam's real happiness was very closely linked with his urge to farm. To deny him that privilege was to doom him to frustration and a sense of futility, competent though he was in his teaching profession. And so there came a day when I exercised voluntary submission and said, "Sure. Let's go farming. I'm with you."

It wasn't an easy thing to say. And there were days of financial stress when I wondered if I had been wise in encouraging him to fulfill so difficult a dream. Except for one thing: despite unbelievably hard work and much smaller dollar returns than he had ever known, Cam was happier than he had ever been before.

Later, when I felt the need to develop my own dream—

that of writing—it was Cam who gave me the constant encouragement that I needed. It was he who encouraged me to take the risks that were necessary to become an established free-lancer; he who read my manuscripts and contributed incisive criticism. And this in spite of the fact that it often meant macaroni casserole for supper, and holes in the heels of his socks! Thus, submission became a mutual affair.

God's pattern is that of strong, spiritually mature women, understanding the reasons for His injunctions and following them volitionally—and thus entering into the kind of joy which He intends should permeate the marriage relationship. It is strong submission—the giving freely of a fully realized self—which I see taught in the New Testament. From voluntary submission of the wife to the husband will flow the blessings which attend obedience: the harmonious functioning of the family unit; happiness, health, and vitality for the woman who allows herself to be husbanded by one who loves her more than she loves herself; the respect and love of a fulfilled husband.

4

Not Only to the Good and Gentle

BETH IS A BEAUTIFUL, gracious woman whose poise suggests inner strength and serenity. She is a sensitive Christian who came to know the Lord Jesus several years after her marriage. Her husband, Don, is an open atheist, a very harsh man. Beth lives with the little hurts and soul-deep lacerations caused by his tongue which is both unkind and blasphemous. He is domineering and demanding.

Over a period of years, I have marveled at Beth's personal growth in a most difficult marriage. In a situation which would crush or embitter many, Beth has found the joyous adjustment of submission; not a crawling, cringing submission, but one enriched with personal dignity.

The other thing I have seen is something happening gradually, almost imperceptibly, to her husband. Don has softened, just a little, and mellowed. And—although it is almost grudgingly—he does show his deep respect and affection for this wonderful wife. Perhaps someday he will love her Lord as well.

Beth's situation is one of those in which submission is difficult. But she is demonstrating by her life that wifely submission is still God's basic method of reaching into the lives of unconverted husbands. The apostolic command is clear:

37

You wives, be submissive to your own husbands so that even if any of them are disobedient to the word they may be won without a word by the behavior of their wives, as they observe your chaste and respectful behavior (1 Peter 3:1-2, NASB).

The reason for submission is that God has ordained an authority structure for the home which Christians must honor. Thus, we do not submit to our husbands because they are gentle and kind, or good, or godly. But because they are our husbands. And because Jesus Christ is our Lord. Applying this truth to the marriage in which only the wife is a Christian is no easy matter. But neither is it a new problem. It was faced by many, many of the new converts in the early Christian Church. And so there are clear New Testament guidelines for the Christian wife to follow.

Dora and I were having a cup of coffee when she dropped her bomb: "I've decided to leave Bob. I just can't take it any longer." Then came the catalog of troubles. Deep near the heart of the problem was the fact that Bob had made no attempt to understand her new discovery of life in Christ. I sipped my coffee as she outlined all of her reasons for leaving, and then I suggested a few reasons why she should consider staying. "Not because Bob is ideal," I told Dora, "but because you are a disciple of Jesus Christ's." We took a look at 1 Corinthians 7:13,16:

. . . the woman which hath an husband that believeth not . . . if he be pleased to dwell with her, let her not leave him. . . . For what knowest thou, O wife, whether thou shalt save thy husband?

Dora made no verbal commitment. But she went home determined to stick it out. She realizes that, for all his faults, her love to Bob is deep, and her greatest desire is that he will meet Jesus Christ as Lord. Staying with him, submitting to him, is her way of demonstrating the love and power of Jesus within their home.

Many a woman who has found Christ wonders and worries about how best to witness to her husband. God's method is clearly outlined. Live with him. Love him. Respect and obey him. As Ruth Bell Graham has put it:

> The best advice I ever heard given to a woman whose husband was not a Christian was: "Your business is not to make him good but to make him happy!" It's God's business to make him good. You take care of the possible and trust God for the impossible.[1]

A wife who becomes a Christian after marriage needs to be sensitive to the dilemma which she poses to her husband. "I feel sorry for Art," one young wife told me. "He can't figure things out. I'm not the same person he married three years ago." She thought for a moment and then went on: "But even he would have to admit that most of the changes in me are for the better. I'm happier, freer, than I have ever been . . . but still, it confuses him."

Women who suddenly confront their husbands with a demand for vast changes in their life-style should not be surprised by the hostility which they face. For the husband, the wife's changed interests are, in effect, a judgment of his interests as not being good enough. The greatest love and tact and wisdom from the Holy Spirit are needed to assure the husband that he is loved as much as ever, or more; that what the wife really wishes is not to impose a different life-style but to share with him a whole new source of life. In an atmosphere of love and acceptance, any individual is more likely to respond to the love of Christ. Especially a husband.

[1] Ruth Bell Graham, "Husbands, Children and God," *Decision* 8, no. 6 (June 1967): 8.

The non-Christian husband is one kind of marriage complication to which the Word of God applies the same basic principle as we found to be workable in marriages between believers. Another, perhaps an even more difficult problem, is that faced by wives of husbands who have rejected an earlier faith, or slipped away from it.

When Marj and Pete were married, they were the ideal couple in their church. Pete was an exuberant young Christian, one who had met the Lord Jesus Christ in a clear-cut conversion experience a few years prior to marriage. He studied the Word of God daily and shared his discoveries with others. And then one day, three years after their marriage, Pete made a simple announcement which shattered their world: "Marj, I can't believe it any longer. It's just an illusion—one you can accept because you were brought up with it. But I just can't swallow it anymore. And there's no point in being a hypocrite about it."

"What could I do?" Marj told me. "I used to see those women who came alone to church on Sunday mornings, and I vowed that I would marry a man who loved the Lord. I did. But nowadays, when I get a chance to go to church, I go alone.

"It's hardest with the kids. I'm determined they must have a chance to know the truth, but Pete is just as determined that they must not be indoctrinated; they must be left free to decide for themselves. So all I can do is pray. And go on loving him. I'm trying to show him that all there is to Christianity is Jesus Christ. I have laid aside the outward forms of my religion. But Jesus is real to me—more now than ever before—and I cannot deny Him."

Marj told me her story simply, after many months of friendship. She didn't weep. "That's past," she told me. "All there is left is faith." But how deeply this tragedy had cut into her life was something not hard to imagine. "At times, I have almost stopped loving Pete," she said. "I have felt so angry, so resentful that he should do this to me—put me through all this. But I ask the Lord to make me more loving than ever. I believe that God will let me love Pete back to his lost faith in Jesus Christ."

By following the Word of God and obeying the inner guidance of the Holy Spirit, Marj is walking an uncharted road with a sure sense of direction.

Anne faces a different sort of problem: Harold is a pleasant, easy-going fellow. He is even a Christian. But he seems to be very little interested in providing spiritual leadership in the home. "What can I do?" Anne asks herself over and over again. "I'd gladly submit if I had someone to submit to!"

Anne is not alone with this problem. C. S. Lewis in his little classic, *The Four Loves*, speaks of the headship given to the man as "inflicted upon him." He says:

> The sternest feminist need not grudge my sex the crown afforded to it . . . for [it is] . . . of thorns. The real danger is not that husbands may grasp . . . [it] too eagerly; but that they will allow or compel their wives to usurp it.[2]

For the woman who is married to a man who will not exercise his headship, the concept of submission is vastly complicated. She needs to carefully assess, if she can, some of the reasons for his shrinking from this responsibility. If it is because, way down deep, he feels insecure or insufficient for the task, her daily respect, love, and acceptance may help to build him up in personal strength to the point where he does take the lead.

There are men who fail to take leadership in the home because they fear friction if they attempt to assert themselves. The wife who is able to communicate her willingness to fol-

[2] C. S. Lewis, *The Four Loves* (New York: Harcourt, Brace & World, 1960), p. 149.

low her husband's lead will encourage him in accepting his role. Many men who would not seize the leadership will take it when it is left to them. Only when a husband has proven that he cannot—or will not—lead, should the wife exercise that abdicated leadership.

The non-Christian husband, the backslidden husband, the passive husband—certainly these present complications in God's pattern for the home. And we have not begun to catalog the kinds of complexities faced by women within marriage. What of those with unfaithful husbands? With non-providing husbands?

The Word of God gives directions with regard to ending untenable marriage relationships. Divorce, in God's order, is reserved as the right of a wronged person when fidelity has been broken (Matthew 5:31-32). God does not require that you live with an unfaithful partner—if you can't. For the act of adultery actually annuls the marriage bond, breaching the "one flesh" union. Yet Jesus made it clear that God never meant for divorce, with all of its heartache and rending, to be a part of the human experience. It was only "because of the hardness of your hearts" (Matthew 19:8) that an "out" from marriage was ever provided in the laws of the Old Testament. And, as Jesus stressed in the Sermon on the Mount, that "out" was to be used only in the case of infidelity. It is an option for the offended party. On the other hand, if a woman can accept the grace from God to go on loving a husband who has been unfaithful, and thus to rebuild her marriage, more power to her.

Mary Henderson found that kind of strength from the Lord. When her husband committed adultery with his secretary, he lost his job. Naturally enough, since he was the pastor of a church. Mary had ample grounds for divorce. She chose instead to stay with John, helping him find a new life to replace the calling he had lost. For many years he was bitter and unrepentant. But against all the odds, Mary stuck with him and raised a family of sons to be outstanding Christian men. And then, twenty-five years after the sin that had rocked their marriage, John melted before the Spirit of God and found forgiveness and full restoration. Today that couple is again finding a place of ministry. Mary's love and determination were successful in salvaging not just a marriage but a man.

Besides infidelity, the only other case in which the New Testament allows for the dissolution of a marriage is when an unbelieving partner packs up because of the difference which has come into the home through the faith of the believer: "If the unbelieving depart, let him depart" (1 Corinthians 7:15).

Basically, however, Christians are to view marriage as a life-long commitment—no matter how difficult it may be. Our culture makes it increasingly easy to consider separation and divorce as a way out of marital difficulties. But God has spoken: "I hate divorce" (Malachi 2:16, NASB). No matter how attractive the chance to escape marital difficulties may be, Christian women will look to God for the strength and grace they need to work out creative solutions within the framework of commitments already made.

5

Love

OUR GOOD FRIEND, Father O'Donnell, sat a little forward in his big chair. "How do you describe heaven in such a way that people really want to go there?" He threw the question out to the discussion group.

I took a stab at it. "I think heaven's a bit like marriage."

"You mean marriage is a bit like heaven?" Father O'Donnell quipped.

"No—that's not what I meant. Although it is," I concurred. "What I meant was this: when I was a young girl, I didn't think I would ever get married. It looked like a bad deal. I mean, on the surface, I can't even yet think of too much to attract a woman to marry." I turned to Christine, a middle-aged single woman, highly professional in her career. "Would you really like to stay at home and wash the floors and make the meals and wipe the dishes?"

Chris laughed. "Hardly. But you have a reason to do it."

"Right. Marriage didn't appeal to me at all, on general principle, until I met Cam. And when I knew I loved him, I wanted to live with him—and that makes marriage a joy."

Christine saw the analogy. "So you can't make a person keen to get to heaven until he first loves God?"

"Right. To me, heaven means being with Jesus Christ forever. And I love Him—so I look forward to that. But I'm not sure that living with God can look so very attractive to anyone who hasn't really fallen in love with Him first."

The discussion roamed on from there, but the analogy is true in reverse too. To be attractive—indeed, to be workable at all—marriage must be motivated by and undergirded with love, the kind of love that makes two people long to live together. Not just to go to bed together, but to get up together too. To face life together morning after morning for a lifetime. Nothing short of this kind of love will be strong enough or elastic enough to survive all the tests of two people living together. It must be love that is more than a mushy tapioca-pudding kind of emotion. It has to be love that is strong and firm. And flexible. Love that wants the best for someone else more than it wants the best for oneself. Love that gives. That is the kind of love that must kindle and constantly fuel a marriage if there is to be any warmth, any joy, any flame there.

Principle 3: Love

Love is the third of the three great New Testament marriage principles. Thus far we have looked at the principles of mutual submission and voluntary submission. But without love, neither is really possible. Here's what the New Testament has to say about married love:

> Husbands, love your wives, even as Christ also loved the church and gave himself for it (Ephesians 5:25).
> Husbands, love your wives, and be not bitter against them (Colossians 3:19).

And this interesting admonition to older women in the church:

> Teach the young women . . . to love their husbands (Titus 2:4).

Now this word "love" needs to be clarified and redefined. In the last decade, we have been swamped with so many declarations of "love" that it has come to mean everything from "like" to "lust." In the name of "love" many shoddy substitutes are being marketed to young people. The phrase *make love* has come to mean "have sexual intercourse."

Of course, in the Christian view of things, sex is a vital and integral part of marriage love. Sex is one of God's good gifts to humanity. I see it as one of the proofs that "God is love." If you doubt that the Bible affirms the joy of sex, you should reread the Song of Solomon. In its poetical and figurative language, it is lyrical about sex in marriage. "Let my beloved come into his garden, and eat his pleasant fruits," the bride invites. "I am come into my garden," the groom replies, "I have gathered my myrrh with my spice; I have eaten my honeycomb with my honey" (Song of Solomon 4:16; 5:1). And it is in this little manual of married love that one of literature's classic definitions of love is found:

"Love is as strong as death,
Jealousy is as severe as Sheol;
Its flashes are flashes of fire,
The very flame of the LORD.
"Many waters cannot quench love,
Nor will rivers overflow it;
If a man were to give all the riches of his house for love,
It would be utterly despised."
Song of Solomon 8:6-7, NASB

While Paul's experiences do not seem to have left him with much enthusiasm about marriage (Pollock suggests that perhaps Paul's unbelieving wife left him after his conversion[1]), he nonetheless endorses both marriage and sex-

[1] John Pollock, *The Apostle: A Life of Paul* (New York: Doubleday, 1969), pp. 37ff.

ual communion within it. "It is better to marry than to burn" (1 Corinthians 7:9), Paul concedes, with a tacit admission of both the reality and legitimacy of sexual passion. And it is Paul who, speaking in the wider context of the Church, gives us another classic definition of love:

> Love is patient, love is kind, and is not jealous; love does not brag and is not arrogant, does not take into account a wrong suffered, does not rejoice in unrighteousness, but rejoices with the truth; bears all things, believes all things, hopes all things, endures all things (1 Corinthians 13:4-7, NASB).

Thus, while sexual passion is certainly a part of married love, it is not the whole of it. We really need to restore the word "love" to its fullest meaning. The massive *Oxford English Dictionary* devotes four of its huge, three-column pages to defining this word! But the primary definition it offers is this:

> LOVE: That disposition or state of feeling with regard to a person which (arising from recognition of attractive qualities, from instincts of natural relationship, or from sympathy) manifests itself in solicitude for the welfare of the object, and usually also in delight in his presence and desire for his approval; warm affection, attachment.

Putting that precise definition together with Scripture and experience makes it possible for us to sharpen our understanding of the nature and expression of love, particularly in marriage.

LOVE IS AN EMOTION

That love is an emotion, a feeling, is the very fact which makes love hard to define and sometimes even hard to rec-

47

ognize. Like other emotions, the "feeling" of love is one which may wax or wane with physical strength, with adverse or pleasant circumstances. Maturing love is one which moves from being merely an emotion to becoming a stable and basic fact in life—thus ceasing to be merely a feeling and becoming a commitment. The overdependency on an emotional aspect of love has resulted in much of the present impermanence of marriage relationships. Consider the sort of emotional love which is sung about in the rock songs of the day, and you will understand how weak and changeable a thing love is as a mere emotion.

Marriage love needs to mature beyond the *feeling* until it becomes a *fact*. When I say, "I love Cam," I may or may not feel any special emotion. But I am stating an emotional fact on which I have built my marriage. I am declaring, not just a come-and-go feeling, but a commitment of my intellect and will to the fact that I love him. Love, then, begins as feeling but matures into fact.

Love is directed outward, toward an object

While self-esteem is a necessary component in sound personality, love on which marriage can be built is love which reaches away from self, toward the loved one. Marriage love is, quite simply, unselfishness. In some marriages "I love you" really means "I love to have you love me." In other cases "I love you" can be most correctly interpreted as "I love me and you love me too."

That's the way it was with Ellen and Joe. If it hadn't been so pathetic, it would have been almost funny to watch Joe's efforts to please Ellen—a woman so selfish she couldn't even please herself! Over a period of a few early marriage years, Joe discovered the one-way street he was on and just simply gave up. Love ceased to be an active ingredient in their marriage.

Not long ago Ellen met the Lord Jesus Christ in a personal encounter. Gradually, as He transforms her, she is changing in her attitude toward Joe. Christ has corrected that fixation of love and interest in herself, and turned it outward—first toward Himself, and then toward others.

Self-love is not the stuff of which enduring marriages can be built. Love must be directed toward someone else. And that requires the grace of God. "Beloved, let us love one another: for love is of God" (1 John 4:7). Real love goes beyond desiring the loved one for the pleasure and comfort he brings to oneself, and loves him just for himself.

LOVE ARISES FROM THE RECOGNITION OF ATTRACTIVE QUALITIES

Whether love is at first sight, or second, or at two hundred and second sight, it comes into being because there is a dawning of recognition of attractive qualities in the other person. "First sight" love can arise only from the recognition of physical attractiveness, but certainly it can lead to mature love if initial physical attraction is backed up by the recognition of deeper-based attractive qualities.

When Mary and Walter were married, they knew each other only very superficially. They felt they had enough in common on which to found a marriage. But by the end of the first year, they were both very disillusioned. "Walter is so dull," Mary sighed. "He just doesn't catch on quickly."

"How could I have known Mary would be so moody?" Walter wondered.

For a few months it looked as though the marriage would founder or else settle into a lifetime of mutual misery. And then a miracle happened. This couple, who had married on the basis of rather superficial attraction, began to discover the deeper attractive qualities of each other. The next time I talked with them, the tone was entirely different.

"Walter finds studying plenty hard," Mary confided. "But, boy, has he got what it takes when it comes to perseverance!"

Walter spoke admiringly too. "Mary is just a born organizer. She helps me in so many ways."

A year and a half after their wedding day, this couple really discovered love—love that arises from realizing the attractive qualities of one another and majoring on them.

LOVE GOES FROM DELIGHT AND DESIRE TO SOLICITUDE AND CONCERN

Love goes beyond solicitude for the object's welfare, to delight in his presence, and desire for his approval—that's the way the dictionary puts it. But my experience just reverses that order to something more like "love goes beyond delight in the loved one's presence . . . to solicitude for his welfare."

Back in those far-off days when I was dating, I found that I was very unconcerned about punctuality on the part of most of my dates. It just didn't matter to me, or with most of them, whether they arrived on time or not. With some of them, it didn't matter to me whether or not they arrived at all. But when Cam was five minutes late, I was frantic, angry, upset—responses which, by the way, hardly earned me his approval. I found it hard to analyze those powerful, almost uncontrollable, emotions then; but now I understand them. I cared for Cam's company. I delighted in his presence. I yearned to be with him. And even temporary delays were hard to accept.

Now, with love maturing, I find myself with other emotions when Cam keeps me waiting. I am still sometimes upset. But, more often now, my response is that of solicitude. How has he been delayed? What complications and frustrations is he facing?

50

LOVE IS A PRODUCT OF, AND IS PRODUCTIVE OF, DEEPENING RESPECT

Here we go beyond the dictionary, as love will always do. "Emotional respect" might be as good a definition as any of love. I can think of two marriages which illustrate love as respect.

Ron and Lenora are nearing their fortieth wedding anniversary. She is an emotional woman, always excited, exuberant, or angry about something. He is the most even, steady man I have ever met. "A Rock of Gibraltar," as one friend says. They are hardly the hand-holding variety of married couple. In fact, although I know them well, I have never seen them exchange so much as a dry little kiss. And that, of course, should mark their marriage as a failure. But their marriage is not a failure. Lenora storms about Ron's slowness sometimes, but she is full of pride and respect at his steady evenness. Ron loves to tease Lenora, but his smile is always gentle. For he, too, is proud of his mate. She is an intelligent and aware woman, and a gifted homemaker. They share their pride in grown sons and daughters and growing grandchildren. This marriage is a success story. It is the permanent, unbreakable bond between two people who are very, very different, but who respect each other deeply.

Tom and Betty, on the other hand, are fairly new at the marriage game. They have been married for only five years, and their courtship was marked by their being very much "in love." Educational plans were ditched to make way for an early marriage. But affectionate as they may have been, there are serious signs of strain in this marriage. Betty shows her disrespect for Tom in little, belittling snubs, and he responds in kind. For their marriage to succeed, they need not so much to fall back in love as to develop respect.

Back of our farm home is a depression, which, each

spring, fills up with water from melting snow. And since this area becomes full about the same time that ducks begin to arrive, usually one or two pairs choose our pond as a nesting site. I am always apprehensive to see them settle in, for the pond is not fed by any permanent streams. By the time the hot suns of summer shine, there is no water left in our pond. The ducks find their nests are high and dry. Reluctantly, they move away to begin again.

Often, as I have watched another spring's supply of unwary ducks move in, I have thought of friends who have built their marriages on a kind of love, or a concept of it, which is not fed from the eternal streams of God's love. Sooner or later the human love drawn only from the attractions of youth begins to dry up. The resources they need for daily renewing their marriage just evaporate under the heat and pressure of day-to-day living.

The idea of "love" within Christian marriage draws its chief pattern from the love of God. Thus, Christian love is—although at best clouded—a mirror of God's great self-giving, unending love. The ultimate expression of that love is seen at Calvary when the Lord Jesus Christ gave Himself for the Church. And it is exactly this moment of divine love, totally without parallel, which Paul points to as the example for married love (Ephesians 5:25-29).

It is illuminating in considering the kind of love which a marriage needs, to consider just what is meant by the phrase "husband." In earlier usage, the word "husband" included the concept of one who cultivated the soil and cared for it. The double concept of husband—both as the married mate and as the tiller of the ground—is found throughout the Old Testament. Through the prophets, God declared Himself to be Husband in both senses to the nation of Israel (cf. Isaiah 54:5; Jeremiah 3:14; Hosea 2:19-20). Not only is He bound to that nation as a Lover, but also as a Keeper. "Now will I sing to my wellbeloved a song of my beloved touching his vineyard. My wellbeloved hath a vineyard in a very fruitful hill: And he fenced it, and gathered out the stones thereof, and planted it with the choicest vine" (Isaiah 5:1-2).

And really, in the best of marriages, this is the kind of husbanding that is required: the careful cultivation of all that is good, the tending of the garden in which mutual respect and love can grow. The man who exercises his prerogatives as a husband will be one who helps his wife to come to fruition as an individual. In doing so, he will reap a harvest of joy and satisfaction for himself.

I came to understand this role of my husband only through one of the hardest lessons I have ever been taught by the Lord. Although I had grasped in theory the concept of voluntary submission, our marriage was far more characterised by mutual submission. And then one year I made a number of commitments in complete disregard of my husband's expressed wishes. Not that he actually forbade them, of course. But he questioned my wisdom; I questioned his questioning and went ahead. It was not very many months before the burden of responsibilities which I had accepted simply crushed me. Ill with exhaustion, I had to lay aside, one by one, the various activities I had entered into. Finally, I had no responsibilities left except caring for my husband and children. And even that seemed, many days, to be beyond my strength.

But gradually my health returned, through months of rest and complete withdrawal from the demanding community. When at last I did feel able to again do some of the extra things which I so enjoyed undertaking, I kept a very simple rule of thumb and observed it rigidly: I refused to accept any task without consulting Cam about it.

A weakling? A coward? Unable to make decisions on my own? I don't think so. Rather, I had learned that decisions which I made most often reflected my own unwillingness to

53

disappoint or let down the friend who asked. Decisions made in consultation with Cam were based on our own overriding interests, the demands of the family, and my health. Very simply, my husband is far better at husbanding my physical resources than I am. He loves me more than I love myself, understands my long-range goals very clearly, and so is better able to sort out obstructions from stepping-stones. His husbandry has enriched my own creative output by pruning away the "suckers" that sap my energy but do not yield any fruit.

"Making love" is a lot more than enjoying sex together. To "make love"—love that is strong as death, love that burns throughout marriage as an unquenchable flame—is a lifelong challenge. To "make love" is to create within a marriage a strong and sweet and, above all, a growing and maturing factor in the relationship between two people. To *really* "make love" and to keep it alive and vital: this is a task which will take all you've got—and give you all that matters in return.

6

Economics of Togetherness

"IF I WERE A MAN," Donna told me, "I would most certainly marry. How else could I get my laundry done, my floors scrubbed, my meals cooked, and my bed warmed—all at no expense?"

She was a young woman, voicing the common complaint of "economic servitude" for women which, we are told by many voices today, is a component of the traditional marriage pattern. This slave-wife concept can be traced to Friedrich Engels, colleague of Karl Marx. "The modern individual family," said Engels, "is founded on the open or concealed slavery of the wife."[1]

Engels' statement is echoed, with reverberations, by other, more modern, writers. Germaine Greer says, "If women are to effect a significant amelioration in their condition it seems obvious they must refuse to marry. No worker can be required to sign on for life; if he did his employer could disregard all his attempts to gain better pay and working conditions."[2]

Economist John Kenneth Galbraith speaks of women being maintained as an unpaid servant caste for the purpose of ad-

[1] Friedrich Engels, *Origin of the Family*, as quoted in "The Discussion Club," *The United Church Observer*, June 1972, p. 53.
[2] Germaine Greer, *The Female Eunuch*, as quoted in ibid.

ministering consumption of the products of our economy. He comments: "Menial employed servants were available only to a minority of the pre-industrial population; the servant-wife is available, democratically, to almost the entire present male population."[3]

We have already given consideration to the scriptural explanation of the origin of the family. The "modern individual family" is an idea which grew in the heart of God before he transplanted it to the Garden of Eden. It is not a product of the Fall, but antedates the Fall. To accept any lower view of the family, suggested by communist or evolutionary frames of thought, is to miss the love plan for human happiness which is behind all of God's gifts to man.

Now I am not for a second suggesting that there cannot be cultural variations on the basic themes, but the themes of marriage as conceived by God remain constant: man and woman together creating an atmosphere of love and mutual submission; woman voluntarily accepting God's order and submitting to her loving, Christlike husband; children finding themselves wrapped in the love of their parents and thus in the love of God.

But we who think seriously about the data which confronts us must ask, "Is slavery necessarily implied by economic dependence?" And the answer is, of course, a most emphatic "No." No doubt there are cases in which slavery is imposed on women through the means of male economic power. But it is not that way in our marriage—nor in numbers of other marriages I could tell you about. We're right back to the conclusions of our last chapter: love is the principle that wipes out the obligations, the servitude, and even the drudgery. Certainly love elevates the relationship

[3] John Kenneth Galbraith, "The Economics of the American Housewife," *The Atlantic Monthly* 232, no. 2 (Aug. 1973): 78ff.

of man and wife above the employer-employee paradigm suggested by Engels, Greer, and Galbraith.

Within a loving framework, both earning and nonearning partners in a traditional marriage are expressing their love to each other. The husband is expressing his love by supporting the family, meeting its needs by "the sweat of his brow." I become highly impatient with the euphoric picture of the workaday world which has been painted by radical feminists. For I have been a part of that "glamorous" world: the nine-to-five, day-after-day, year-in-and-year-out routine. No amount of romanticizing can make a job something else than work. No matter how engrossing, how challenging, how remunerative, any person who is bound to a job is in just as great "slavery" as the person who stays at home.

Not many years ago, my husband needed to take a leave of absence from his teaching position for some pressing business. Our teaching credentials were identical, so I hired a baby-sitter and stepped in for him for a couple of months. I won't deny how eager I was to try out my career again. But if ever I had envied him his work (and I had!), the envy was gone by the end of my stint. I was exhausted. I was weary of facing job routines. A friend asked me if I enjoyed being back at work. "Not for long at a time," I confessed. "I'm too liberated to want a job."

It is, then, an act of love for the husband to accept the servitude of a job. (And let's face it, there are probably just as many men in jobs they don't especially like as there are women who are unhappy in their role at home.) It is completely untrue to suggest that the man who supports his family is free while his wife is in slavery.

Equally, it is an act of love for the woman to create a home. From time to time I have had temporary house help, often teenage girls. I find that the work for a family of six simply boggles their minds. "I would never have believed it," one girl panted at the end of the first week. "There is no end to the work!" And that with the help of every modern appliance. Another girl became increasingly resentful about her work. I tried to find out the problem. "It's just that nobody really says thank you," she said finally.

I reminded her about the many times when I had thanked her—sincerely—for I have always been grateful to those who have helped in the house. And then, as we discussed the problem, she realized that it was the work itself that was thankless. "Sheila," I said quietly, "someday you will gladly do for love what now you cannot like to do for money."

She was married the other day to a fine Christian man, and I am certain that my prediction will be fulfilled. For love takes the unpleasantness out of routines. There's nothing very challenging about sorting wash, perhaps. But that pair of socks belongs to Geoff, and here's the little shirt that Mitchell spilled his orange juice on. And Cam's work pants—greasy and grimy—that have brought him more pleasure than all the fine wool worsted pants he ever wore while teaching school. And so for me there is meaning in a "menial task."

I cannot see how "slavery" of the wife can be implied by the earning power of the husband unless the husband is selfish and unsharing with his resources. Clearly, if a wife has to cringe and scrape for what should be hers without question, then there is something wrong. But in a fair and loving marriage, the husband makes his resources fully available to the wife, and the wife is equally unselfish in the management of those resources. In love, one supplies the earnings from his work; the other supplies services. And far from being an independent-dependent relationship between husband and wife, it is a mutually understood state of interdependence.

As far as I can see, sharing fully in the husband's earnings is the only way in which the labor of a housekeeping wife is properly valued. The idea that the wife renders services for which she is not paid is really false—unless the husband withholds support. The man who loves his wife shares all he has—however much or little—not considering his resources to be his, but theirs. And thus he recognizes the value to him of having a homemaker. Not that he pays her for her services. Heaven forbid! I refuse to be turned into either a professional housekeeper or a prostitute by such a concept.

Rightly viewed, economic dependency can mean the exact opposite of slavery—and probably does to the truly emancipated woman. It can mean freedom. As has been pointed out, the workaday world is a kind of bondage too. But the supported wife is one of the few members of our society who has been freed from the battle for bread for other more meaningful pursuits. Let us not be brainwashed by the propaganda which suggests that only dollar-valued activities are significant. Even if society as a whole should become so ill that it can no longer value the freely given hand of help, the volunteer labor of love, the cultivation of a home atmosphere of love and peace, the development of good minds, surely we who are Christians should be free enough in our thinking to recognize such values.

While it is true that in the early years of family establishment a woman has little time and much distraction, as the years pass, a woman who does not need to hold a job can be a free woman in a sense which few liberationists can begin to understand.

Up to this point, I have been stressing that the economic principle of marriage is one of interdependence. Really, that is why two people marry in the first place. They realize that they need each other. They sense that they are dependent upon each other emotionally and, in marriage, widen that interdependence. Whether a couple follows the traditional marriage pattern of male as income-earner and female as service-provider, or whether, for at least some periods dur-

59

ing their marriage, both partners are earners and both share in providing services, the key to harmony will be admission of this interdependence and its concomitant need for specialization.

Certainly I don't think there is any reason why the husband shouldn't cook meals—if that's his thing. Nor is there any scriptural reason that I know of why the wife shouldn't do the mechanical work on the car—if that's her thing. But in the interests of efficiency, they should not both be cluttering their minds with meal preparation and car overhauling. I think that we can accept widely variant specializations; and we will, I am sure, see more and more experimentation with role change among younger couples. But, really, the key concept in role differentiation is specialization. And the idea that both partners should share in every aspect of marriage seems to me to be a very inefficient and ineffective way of working within the structure. The decision as to specializations will come through experience and discussion. It should be based on mutual preferences, individual abilities, and special interests. It should be flexible and nondictatorial. But specialization needs to exist to free both members of the partnership to do a good job of what they undertake.

There is no question that economic arrangements within marriage remain as an area of great tension. Careful discussion and joint planning are necessary to prevent misunderstandings from arising. Probably the most important element of fiscal management is respect for the basic dignity of each partner; neither partner should be made to feel inferior—either as a provider or a disperser. Each needs some money to call his or her own . . . money which does not have to be accounted for penny by penny. In a monthly budget, a set amount for "personal allowance"—possibly equal for the home-staying and outgoing partner—should be enough to cover personal incidentals. How much that allowance can be will be determined by the overall budget. But the free spending of even a small amount of money on a regular basis—the right to a small spree—is a healthy safety valve within a marriage.

Then, too, it probably makes sense for each partner to administer some of the earnings in the areas in which they specialize. She may do the best job of buying groceries and children's clothes. He might well look after car repairs, home payments, and utilities. But, of course, it need not be done that way. If either partner is gifted in administering money—making it get all the way around with maybe even a little left over—it makes only good sense to let that one administer funds—whether it be the man or the woman.

Barefoot? Is that how a woman should be? Sure—if she wants to be. But not barefoot because she is inferior, bowing and scraping before her master. Barefoot because it is comfortable to be that way. Not barefoot, either, because her husband deprives her of life's necessities. For they are "heirs together," not only of the grace of the next life, but of the good things of this life too. She relates to him, recognizing their interdependence and need for mutual submission to each other, as well as her place of voluntary submission.

Barefoot? Perhaps it has a new meaning to us now. Do you remember Moses at the burning bush? "Put off thy shoes from off thy feet," God's voice said, "for the place whereon thou standest is holy ground" (Exodus 3:5). I think that's how I feel about it. If, in my heart, I am a barefoot wife, it is because I recognize the God-sanctified nature of marriage. For me, marriage is holy ground, made so in creation by God's loving design, made so in history by Jesus' sociable presence, but especially for me, made so by His own gracious presence in our home.

Yes, I stand on holy ground, and if my feet are bare it is out of reverence for the One who showed us how to love in such a way that holy ground is great to stand on.

Part 2

NURTURE—and Be Free

7

A Christian View of Motherhood

ONE OF THE MOST TERRIFYING elements of Huxley's predictive *Brave New World* is the destruction of the family by a technological society. In order to destroy the old values of familial relationships, children of that society are brainwashed until they consider "mother" a dirty word. Another antiutopian prophecy is Orwell's *1984*. In this book, a totalitarian regime works to prevent family ties from becoming binding in any way; motherhood is considered a duty to the state, but children are taught to disrespect and hurt their parents in every possible way.

Both prophecies are being fulfilled in our world today: Orwell's in the giant communist totalitarian states, Russia and China; Huxley's in our own technological society. In the communist societies, the state absorbs all aspects of individual life, including family life. Women are encouraged to work—in part by the near impossibility of a family existing on one worker's earnings, but also by a continuous propaganda program which treats nonworking women as the lazy, indolent, nonproductive members of a "workers' society." In China, the forces against motherhood in any of its traditional meanings except childbirth is even stronger. Women must work. Children are placed in day-care centers, where the state's values can be passed on to them at a very early age. The role of mother as chief imprinter of values has been effectively destroyed.

And what of our own society? Increasingly the thought waves of this continent are dominated by those who demand as a "right" that women go out to work. What about a woman's right to be a mother—not merely in a biological sense, but in a true sociological sense? This right seems about to be denied to many women for whom it is, indeed, a route to fulfillment and satisfaction. Day-care centers are demanded so that women can return to the work force with a minimum of delay after giving birth. What of the evidence that the early preschool years are the most significant in the shaping of character, implanting of values? This data seems to have been firmly set aside in the struggle to "liberate" women from the home. But there are questions which must be raised. Do all women really want to be freed from the cultural tasks of motherhood? And should Christian women even ask to be so freed?

The Zero Population Growth people have made their case so plain that many young mothers have felt, as I have, the castigation of others if they presume to have more children than that prescribed number: two. So that while "mother" has not quite become a dirty word, we are well on the way to denigrating the purposefulness and meaning of the woman functioning as a mother, to denying the right of responsible parents to any more than two children. But we must not let these constantly paraded ideas press us into the world's way of thinking. As Christians, our task is to discern the mind of God with regard to parenthood—something discussed in greater depth in the next chapter.

The thing that is most serious about the constant attacks on the meaningfulness of motherhood is that it affects the thinking of women in one of the most vulnerable periods of their lives. Young motherhood—and I've been there—is a time of enormous weariness. Interrupted sleep brings about a tiredness that goes so deep the bones ache with it. Black circles form under the eyes, and one day the young mother looks into the wan reflection in the kitchen mirror and asks bleakly, "Where has my youth gone?" She finds that she has been changed by the experience of motherhood, that her vivacity and buoyancy, even her intellectual curiosity, have largely disappeared while she has ground through days and nights of changing diapers, preparing formula, answering cries.

At such a moment, the woman is highly vulnerable to the siren voices of the liberationists. "Anatomy is not destiny," the voices echo all around her. "You don't really need to bear children or, having borne them, let them determine your life-style. Why waste your youth in such meaningless activity?" And the young mother sometimes—almost—finds herself joining in the resentment against the biological functions of her body. Almost. But she knows that such resentment is rebellion against the God who made her as He did. And she recalls her glad acceptance of being a woman: made in God's image equally with man, but so very different from man. She remembers the triumph of childbirth, and she reaches down to feel the grasp of her baby's tiny fingers on her own chapped hand. And she knows that they are wrong—those women who tell her that nothing can be worth so much of her life.

She knows that to give children life she must give of her own life. And knowing that, she gives gladly. Sometimes she is discouraged. Always, tiredness seems closer than her own skin. But she knows that this motherhood business is not just something that has happened to her; it is part of her life that is real, and big, and intimately linked to basic meanings.

The young mother, too, is vulnerable to the voices of the would-be emancipators, because her own career has been at least temporarily set aside, and she knows a measure of frustration in this. Her husband pursues his career. She stays home and wipes noses. Of course it is unfair, she sometimes feels. And the voices all around are calling to her: "Chuck it, girl. Call in a baby-sitter and get on with living." And then she remembers that living is more than working; living is more than making a career, even. Living is sometimes giving—the deep, deep giving which is motherhood. And she rejects the voices which invite her to virtual child abandonment, refusing it as the voice of the tempter.

But the young mother's vulnerability is perhaps greatest in her hours of depression. Depression is the common lot of young mothers. Post-partum "blues" are listed as a fact of childbirth recovery in every baby manual I have read. These blues are caused by a whole set of factors: emotional tension, fatigue, hormone imbalance. But after-baby blues are not the only sieges of depression which young women must withstand. Betty Friedan thought she had discovered the cause of this malaise of depression in the purposelessness of housewifery.[1] There can be no question but that the woman who centers her whole meaning in either housewifery or children is doomed to great disillusionment, and hence depression. I think the real cause of the depression faced by so many young women is partly physical and partly emotional. Bone-deep weariness is depressing in itself. And on top of that is the emotional drain of continuous demands. Any mother who has had several preschoolers to care for at once understands what I mean.

And yet, even in depression, the Christian woman has an advantage over those who do not know Christ. She is able to offer motherhood, as all other aspects of her life, as a sacrifice of love to her Master. She is able to pour out her cup of depression as a libation, turning it into the "sacrifice of praise." She is aware that God created her with the capac-

---

[1] Betty Friedan, *The Feminine Mystique*, pp. 272ff.

ity—psychological as well as anatomical—for mothering. And she enters into that role as an act of love for Him who called her.

It is with her eyes firmly fixed on Jesus, her identity fully realized in Him as an individual of worth and stature, that she is able to repudiate the voices that call to her. She rejects both the sweet, syrupy voices of those who tell her to make motherhood her total life, and the harsh, strident voices of those who invite her to liberate herself from motherhood's demands.

The Spirit-taught young woman who seeks to follow the teachings of Scripture with regard to motherhood will find ample guidelines: mothers whose names shine like stars in the dark night of history. *Sarah*, who named her promised baby, born in her old age, "Laughter," explaining, "God hath made me to laugh, so that all that hear will laugh with me" (Genesis 21:6). Laugh with Sarah—of course! The old woman who had craved a child all her life, suddenly swelling with a child—*the* child—enabled to bear that child, then nursing him at her breast. Oh the joy! And I love that beautiful old woman for the laughter in it all. The sheer amazement, incredulity, delight, and glee at becoming a mother— here's a good cure for young-mother depression!

And there is *Jochabed*, listed among the heroes of faith in Hebrews 11 for her courageous and decisive action in saving the life of her condemned baby boy, Moses. He was a "goodly child" (Exodus 2:2). Can't you just imagine the bloom on him as he filled out? The solid, smoothly plump little limbs, and the pretty pink mouth puckering and unpuckering in sleep—he was "a goodly child." She could not let him die at the whim of a wicked king. And so she hid him for three months. What ingenuity she must have used, and how well-trained her two older children must have been. Then Jochabed launched her little son, in faith, on the Nile River, launched him on a career that would be unmatched

69

in Israel's history. And so Moses' mother's faith is credited alongside his own in God's catalog (Hebrews 11:23).

Read about *Hannah* of the broken heart and yearning prayer, of the promise before her child's birth that he would be given to the Lord "all the days of his life" (1 Samuel 1:11). What a woman Hannah was! There is about her a tenderness blended with determination and firmness that is most admirable. She made a vow which would knife her own heart. And when her little boy was three years old, she fulfilled that vow—taking him to the priest to become his apprentice and weeping all the way home. Hannah, who year by year provided a covering for Samuel (1 Samuel 2:19), and so prefigured all of the mothers who would, by faith, claim God's salvation for their children until they would reach the age of accountability and receive Jesus Christ as their own Lord and Saviour.

Consider *Mary*. I do not find it so amazing that she was worshiped by the medievalists. For in that hour when the birth pangs came, women longed for someone in heaven who had felt that pain and could solicit for them God's aid. The wider Christian view sees God's own love as knowing and encompassing all human suffering, even the pain of travail. But we do not need to worship Mary to respect her for setting aside her own hopes, dreams, and reputation to become the mother of our Lord. And from her we can learn the sweetness of spirit that says, "Behold the handmaid of the Lord; be it unto me according to thy word" (Luke 1:38).

Then there was that marvelous grandmother-mother team, *Eunice* and *Lois*, credited with the early childhood teachings which brought about Timothy's readiness for conversion (2 Timothy 1:5; 3:14-15).

The honorable mention given to such godly mothers as those we have just mentioned coupled with direct teaching in the Bible shows very clearly the value which God places on motherhood. "Lo, children are an heritage of the LORD: and the fruit of the womb is his reward" (Psalm 127:3). Women are reminded in the New Testament that they will "be saved in child bearing" (1 Timothy 2:15)—a particularly obscure passage which I think is best read as an encouragement to women to find their basic ministry within the home.

The importance of motherhood to God can be seen in the extra measure of love which He makes available for the task of motherhood. The experience of "loving children" is not unique to the Christian mother. It is an emotion that comes with motherhood, even for the most depraved. A converted lesbian, Bonnie Hoyum, describes the overwhelming love she felt for her baby daughter, born out of wedlock. "My baby gave me a new determination to straighten out. I loved her so much I would have given my life for her."[2] Here was a person who had violated her own nature, and yet she was endowed with love for her child.

Any place in this world where we find a grain of unselfish love, we see the goodness of God, for such love can come only from Him. It is clear to me that He has stamped motherhood with His giving, undemanding kind of love. It is because God knows how important motherhood is both to us women and to the children we bear that He has thus blessed it with His love.

At this period in history, Satan is spearheading a most insidious and hateful attack against the home, motherhood, and family love. His temptation to women to rationalize their way out of family commitments and responsibilities to children will ultimately rob womanhood of joy and blessing, as surely as his seduction of Eve robbed her. As in the Garden of Eden, his appeal is to our minds. He invites us to

[2] Bonnie Hoyum with Marilyn McGinnis, "I'm Free," *Moody Monthly,* Sept. 1973, pp. 35ff.

look around and check his statements with empirical evidence. He whispers, "Hath God said?" and mocks our timid acceptance of God's order of things. And he invites us to live for ourselves. He doesn't even offer stakes as high as those he held out in the garden. He doesn't need to. We are already fallen creatures, already half ready to give way to his temptation. To Eve he held out the goal, "Ye shall be as gods." To us, he seems to be making good headway by simply suggesting, "Ye shall be as men." If we listen to his subtle offers, we will find ourselves, like Eve, disinherited of the garden of love.

God does not wish us to "be as gods." He has a far higher calling for us: to be like Christ. And He has never intended for us to "be as man." He has something better for those of us who are willing and obedient. We can be ourselves: women.

And, in God's goodness to us: mothers.

8

Vocation to Motherhood

I HAVE FRIENDS in all stages of young marriage: those who are wondering about the whole project of motherhood; those who are wishing for a baby now; those who hope they never have one; and those with new babies—their first, second, or third. And as I talk with these young women, I become increasingly aware that the most important thing about the whole matter of motherhood is that the women who become mothers should have a sense of the rightness of it for them: a desire to be a mother, a knowledge of God's call to motherhood.

"Vocation" is a word which is used a lot. Usually it means a job or career. But its real meaning is *calling*. Vocation, properly understood, is God's call to us. And as in every other decision of major importance, we need to know God's call to motherhood.

His call to biological motherhood will come only to those who have been called to marriage previously. Of course, there is nothing to rule out a single woman's adopting a child if she is assured of her vocation to motherhood on other grounds than marriage. But basically, God's intention is that parenthood should be a shared task. Bearing a child outside of marriage, now declared by some liberationists as a "right" of a single woman, must be rejected. The New

Testament rules out "sex and the single girl" (see Acts 15:29; 1 Corinthians 6:13-19); no Christian woman seeking God's best for her life will assume biological motherhood outside of marriage. (Let's face it, sometimes Christian women do become pregnant outside of marriage. God's love and forgiveness are big enough even for such situations, but coping with motherhood which is a result of disobedience and sin is far from the calling to motherhood which God intends.)

Marriage, then, is the first indication of possible vocation to motherhood. The second indication is a growing instinctual desire to reproduce. This is planted within human nature and becomes stronger with maturity. When a marriage has ripened so that the two have become one, and love has deepened and widened so that it can be shared with a family, then the instinctual desire to reproduce becomes a clear calling.

I remember once, when Cam and I had been married for about two years, we visited friends who had a new baby. I had never been one to cuddle other people's babies, but that evening as I held that tiny infant, a whole new emotion surged through me: an unutterable longing to have a child of my own. The instinctual desire to become a mother was beginning to play its part in preparing me for motherhood. This desire for children, for procreation, for sharing love and life with a new generation, is the natural product of maturation, the outflow of married love. To term it as "mere biology" is to downgrade one of the prime tasks given to the human race by God. Procreation is part of God's purpose, and the instincts which move us toward readiness for procreation are also part of His purpose. The gradual awakening of desire for a child is much like the gradual awakening of desire for a mate. And it happens to almost every woman—both the sweet, demure little girl who played with

74

dolls throughout her young years, and the tough, sturdy tomboy who scorned such pursuits.

A third factor in assessing vocation to motherhood is the physical capability to mother. But here again, it needs to be stressed that motherhood is far more than biological child-bearing. I would encourage the woman who yearns for children but is biologically incapable of bearing her own—if you are sure of your call to motherhood—to make a home for a foster child or, if possible, adopt. You may have to accept into your home a child of mixed race or doubtful genetic heritage; you may have to be willing to accept a child with a disability. But if your love is strong enough and your sense of vocation sure enough, you will find these to be minor obstacles to the expression of yourself in motherhood.

Preparation for motherhood consists of a many-faceted adjustment, and it demands far more than the knitting of dainty little things to fold away in tissue. It was not until the final weeks of my first pregnancy that I settled down to sewing up a layette. (I had spent the earlier weeks writing short stories and articles.) When I took some of the finished items—carefully stitched nighties touched with embroidery—to show a friend, her relief was obvious. "Oh, Maxine," she exclaimed, "they are just lovely. And am I glad to see them. I was beginning to think you had no mother instinct!"

To me, preparation for motherhood meant so much more than those last-minute, precious things. There was the mental preparedness which began with the desire for a child and moved through assessing the meaning of giving up my career. I loved teaching. To me, my career had always meant more than a mere stopgap en route to family founding. I was very professional about my work, and giving up teaching—perhaps forever—was not an easy or automatic decision. But I felt it was a decision which had to be made realistically and honestly. To have merely shrugged it off, or to have postponed consideration of what this would mean to me, would have been to invite myself to live with the nagging problem of indecision. The constant question Shall I go back to work? Now? Later? repeats itself just until one has made a firm decision on the matter.

Then, too, I became deeply aware in those preparation days of the responsibility of bearing children and bringing them up for God. For me, this was a very serious matter.

The need for spiritual preparation may well be one of the reasons God grants us a nine-month gestation period. We need time to adjust ourselves spiritually and mentally to the new demands. Motherhood brings a person to the realization of her deep need of God's help. And, sensing this new dependency, a woman finds herself praising God for a lot of things she never really thought about before. Mary's Magnificat, "My soul doth magnify the Lord" (Luke 1:46) has been echoed through the ages by countless pregnant mothers who feel their babies moving in the womb.

Financial preparedness needs to be considered in making the basic decision to enter into parenthood. I know for myself that with pregnancy came a very strong nesting instinct—a desire to have a place to call our own. Other women have told me of their having the same feeling. Unfortunately, our standard of living has shot up so high that "a place to call our own" can mortgage a lifetime's earnings. This financial burden often encourages young couples to postpone having their families until many years after their marriage. But that nesting instinct can be satisfied without wall-to-wall broadloom and multiple bathrooms. Perhaps there is an old house that can be maintained by tender loving care, or a farmhouse beyond the city limits. A love-filled apartment can satisfy all the basic needs of a child too.

"When I first found I was expecting," Marianne told me, "I was insistent that we build a home. How could we have a family in an apartment? But Bill showed me with pencil and paper that we just could not afford a home, and I came to realize that love and nutrition can be supplied in simple surroundings, right here in our little suite."

It is better to postpone the house than to postpone the baby, for a number of reasons. One is that the chances of genetically sound babies are greatest during the younger childbearing years; another is that the demands of babies (and later, teenagers) require the strength of youth. And, of course, selfishness can creep over a marriage; finally a couple is unwilling to make the necessary adjustments in standard of living, life-style, and habits, to accommodate a family. Becky told me just how difficult she and Roger found it to adjust to their first baby after seven years of childless, carefree marriage. And I shall never forget the wistful voice of a career colleague who told me, "Christmas is mighty lonely when you have no family. You know, we always planned to have a family, but we just kept postponing it until we suddenly realized we were just plain too late."

Physical preparedness for a family also must be considered. A woman needs to realize that while pregnancy seems to have a tonic effect on her general health, buoyant well-being is not the common lot of young mothers with infants making demands night and day. If there are physical problems, a physician's counsel should be sought before a pregnancy is commenced. With proper care, almost any handicap can be overcome, as Marie proved. After a near-fatal car accident, she carried a baby despite severe pelvic and hip damage. She is a proud and radiant mother today.

Then, too, a couple needs to assess their genetic heritage. Where there are serious genetically linked disabilities which they might pass on to another generation, they might have to consider a responsibility not to have children of their own.

The careful preparation of mind, body, spirit, and pocketbook which I have been suggesting has presupposed my endorsation of birth control. And while the topic is almost undebated any longer, Christian leadership and spokesman-ship in the field have been lacking until quite recently. As a teenager, I read in magazines only the opinion of secularists as opposed to that of the Church: the Roman Catholic Church. And having heard no other opinion voiced in my church, I assumed that the Christian stance was against birth control. I am grateful that my attention was steered to Scripture on the matter before I was married. "Defraud not yourselves," Paul said, as we have already noted. To cheat one another of sex within marriage for the purpose of limiting a family seems to me to be far short of God's intention for sex as a source of pleasure and strength within marriage. To have as many children as "come" is unbelievably hard on a woman. Birth control places within the reach of a couple the opportunity of intelligently deciding, before God, the timing and size of their family.

How many children should you have? We are told today that we have no right to more than two children—that we ought not to do more than replace ourselves in a world which is rapidly becoming overcrowded. But God's Word stands: "Be fruitful, and multiply, and replenish the earth" (Genesis 1:28). Now that the earth is quite well "plenished" I don't think anyone needs to feel guilty if they have no children, or only two. But neither should anyone be made to feel guilty who feels that it may well be worth the sacrifices and labor involved to have more than two children. (I have four, you know. I obviously am defending those of us with "big" families!) To me, the questions involved concern the following:

1. Financial ability to support a large family in our very costly society. This does not mean financial ability to give children everything—but an ability to meet their basic needs for shelter, nutrition, clothing, and education.

2. Physical strength. It takes a lot out of a woman to bear children, and the number may well be determined by her health.

3. Mental strength. How many children can you cope with? give yourself to? enrich? teach the Word of God to?

Not only does birth control allow us to determine the number in our families, but also the timing of their births. The first pregnancy should be commenced when the couple's marriage has passed through the difficult early adjustment phase of a year or two. While couples sometimes do have children within the first year of marriage, adjusting both to marriage itself and to a child at the same time places a very heavy emotional strain on both partners. Some delay between marriage and the onset of pregnancy seems to be a good plan, allowing a couple to enjoy the passionate early months of marriage without the complications of pregnancy. Time between births can also be planned. Probably about two years between the birth of each child is optimum —allowing the mother time to recuperate, and yet not letting the difference in children's ages to get too large. However, all kinds of other arrangements work out fine too.

"The best laid schemes o' mice and men gang aft agley," as Scottish poet Robert Burns put it. And such is certainly the case with all birth-control methods. The human element is always there. What happens when you are faced with an unplanned pregnancy? Not a pleasant situation for anyone to be in—least of all, you. The women's libbers shout: "It's your body. Do what you want. If you don't want that pregnancy, abort the fetus." But as a Christian woman you know that "you are bought with a price: therefore glorify God in your body, and in your spirit, which are God's" (1 Corinthians 6:20). While abortion might sometimes be a necessary therapeutic choice, it is reasonable to say that abortion as a means of birth control is not a responsible use of the knowledge God has given. I cannot help but feel that, in the case of the unwanted or unplanned pregnancy, the woman should accept that, over and above her plans, God is sovereign. He may have some very special gift to give her in that unborn child.

An older friend of mine tells me that, years ago, after having three children, she was fitted with a type of I.U.D. Somehow, it didn't quite work. She found herself reluctantly pregnant. But the daughter she bore she calls tenderly her "gold ring baby"—because, through the faulty working of that "gold ring," she was given a beautiful daughter who has been a continuous source of joy. My friend didn't plan for Betty Lou, but there can be little doubt that God did.

In such acceptance, there is the assurance that, finally, joy will be the result. The anticipation of pregnancy and labor is not attractive when it has not been rationally planned for. But "God is able to make all grace abound toward you" (2 Corinthians 9:8), and unplanned pregnancies can be gracefully accepted as from the Lord.

The woman who has prepared herself in mind and spirit for the birth of her child will still find herself amazed at the emotional wonder of bearing a child. Labor is not an event to be feared, but a task to be undertaken "for the joy that . . . [is] set before" (Hebrews 12:2). A positive mental attitude toward labor, coupled with sound prenatal training and reading on the subject, can take much of the apprehension—and some of the pain—out of labor.

The great, marvelous moment of delivery is a moment of psychological and physical exultation which nothing else can match. I couldn't believe how wonderful becoming a mother made me feel, and marveled to a close friend, "Nothing I have ever achieved or could ever achieve could match the pride and joy of this!"

Let me share with you a page from the scrapbook I made

when Geoffrey, our first child, was born. I knew then that the wonder would never be recaptured, so I recorded it while it was all fresh and real.

How can I express the thrill of seeing our firstborn hung aloft by his heels? Of seeing his little purple body flush red? Of hearing a wonderfully strong and deep first cry? There are no words for the waves of joy, relief, and gratitude that surged over me. A son!

As we examined our little boy a few minutes later—observing his straight little nose, his ears exactly like Cam's, his tiny hands perfect replicas of Grandpa Hancock's—our hearts swelled with worship to a Creator who could so marvelously make a child, and make him ours. There in the hospital room, Cam held his son in his arms and together we presented our child to our heavenly Father, asking that his life would bring only glory to God's name. How earnestly we prayed that our wonderful, beautiful little Son of Adam would early, early, become a son of God.

And then Cam was gone, and the baby was gone, and there was rest—deep, sweet rest—for a girl who had, in a wonderful, exultant moment, become a mother.

In those first few days, I had sweet communion with the Lord as He taught me, through this new and profound experience, more about Himself. There were new analogies for me to understand. As I realized how deep was our love for a tiny, helpless infant who had done nothing to deserve our love at all, except to be born into our family, I had a new realization of God's Father love for us, His sons—entirely undeserved, but ours simply because we are His sons!

How new and real became our Lord Jesus Christ's condescension in incarnation. That the great Creator could become the weakest and most helpless of His creatures ... God—in the womb; God—at the breast; God—in diapers!

81

And then, one morning, as I "kept all these things and pondered them in my heart," my heart suddenly overflowed with praise for the whole manner of birth, the whole beautiful pattern. "Trust God," I thought, "to plan such a beautiful way to continue the human race. Trust God to plan that a child should be the result and fruit of love. And thank God He made me a Woman!"

9

Facing the Challenge

"WHAT A WASTE!" A community lady shook her head when I explained that I didn't plan to return to teaching for several years. "All that talent and training, and you stay at home."

As another friend told me, "There was a day when the woman who went back to work was looked at askance. Now it's the other way around. You have to justify staying home!"

This shift in thinking exerts pressures on every young mother which she has to carefully examine if she is to be able to resist them. Despite the casual disclaimers of some vocal women writers, motherhood is far more complex than a mere biological phenomenon. It involves all aspects of personality in the creation of new life. Of course, the concept of motherhood has been smothered with carnations in the past. Our generation rejects sentimentality and demands that a sane, clearheaded look at the task of motherhood be taken.

Several years ago, the students' union of a school where I was teaching brought in an "elocutionist" or monologuist for a "cultural evening." I suppose he was the last of a vanishing line—a man who could support himself by giving recitations of William Henry Drummond, Rudyard Kipling, and Longfellow. After the intermission, he announced that he always did a piece in memory of his mother, long dead. I remember little about the recitation except how dreadful it was; it was embarrassingly mawkish. I felt more embarrassed for his poor mother than anything.

Stock responses to the word "mother" are almost as obnoxious to me as are the radical repudiations of all that the term means. I hope that my children will have a response to me based on the fact that I am a person whom they esteem rather than on some mysteriously conditioned attitude of veneration. But asking that the view of mother be stripped of mystique and sentimentality does not in any way suggest a lower view of the function of motherhood. To my way of thinking, it suggests the opposite. For it allows us to truly evaluate the really important aspects of motherhood, and the significance of the task.

Long after tummy muscles have retautened, the creating of new life goes on. Mothers have been granted the sensitive task of caring for children in their most crucial and fragile years. Of course, this was always meant to be a shared task—God's plan calls for a father and a mother. His plan is for two whole persons working together in procreation and child nurture. But there can be little doubt that the structure which gives to mothers a prime role in shaping the lives of their children is more than just a result of social evolution, as some suggest. Thus it was to be for Adam and Eve: Eve to bear—in pain—her children; Adam to toil—with sweat—for a livelihood for his family. Both the pain and the sweat have been modified, but the roles still bear some resemblance to that primeval pattern.

Someone who loves and cares deeply needs to have the care of children in their early years. And the fulfillment of this function is "mothering." Obviously mothering can be done by other than the biological mother. It can be done by an adoptive mother, by a surrogate such as a nurse, or even—as in some few modern families—by a father. But mothering needs to be done. And I think that most biologi-

cal mothers would probably choose the opportunity of nurturing the creatures whom they expel into the world if they
were given an honest choice.

Today, in the name of liberation, many young women are
finding themselves cheated of one of the tasks which is most
important in womanhood: that of mothering. I know women
who would gladly be home with their little tots except for
outside pressures which dictate that their training shouldn't
be "wasted" in the home; that they will "stagnate" if they
stay out of the labor force. I know others who are wearily
back at work, leaving little infants with sitters because their
husbands demand that they make a financial contribution to
the family. This is liberation? If liberation means being
freed from the very tasks in which we find our greatest happiness and satisfaction, then we had better join the resis-
tance—but fast.

This should not suggest that I am opposed to any shifting
in roles. As industry and professions become more flexible in
hiring practices, we shall probably see more and more
young couples share child nurture about half and half, each
parent working half time. And this will probably come
closer to approximating an ideal pattern than the present
situation in which the woman has almost total responsibility
for child nurture—the husband often leaving in the mornings
before the children are up and returning after they have
been tucked in bed. A study of Scripture places the ultimate
responsibility for child nurture on the father (check me out
in Colossians 3:21; Ephesians 6:4; 1 Timothy 3:12).
Changes in society which restore the father to a more active role in child nurture are real progress. But, while I
gladly share the responsibility with my husband, I wouldn't
really want to turn over the job entirely to him—or to anyone
else.

For the fact is that mothers have vested in them the opportunity of value implantation, cultural and spiritual de-

velopment, and mental and physical development for their children. These are opportunities which can allow for endless creativity and demand the utmost in personal resources of all kinds.

Not that a mother always feels entirely thrilled by all this. As my good friend Doris commented, "I wonder why it always has to be me to answer to 'Mom-my!'" I remember the feeling of frustration and futility that sometimes swept over me in the days—not very long ago—when I was almost endlessly bogged down with diapers, folding, and ironing. And when it seemed that there was always at least one of my brood who was sick. And when the moment-to-moment demands were incessant. For several months I had four children under school age needing my help and guidance and correction and interest. And while I pulled pants up and down, wiped runny little noses, rinsed diapers in the toilet bowl, and read stories for the one-hundredth time, I felt as though I were being left behind by the mainstream; my professional skills were lying dormant. Besides, we were experiencing the financial pressures common to young families. The temptation to go back to work was constant; the opportunity ever present.

But every once in a while I sat down and relisted for myself my life goals which I had defined many years earlier, even before I had children. (Have you ever made such a list? It has been a great help to me in keeping short-range interests from interfering with lifelong goals. It helps, too, in directing energies toward areas which are most meaningful.) Anyhow, my own personal list looked like this:

OVERRIDING LIFE AIM: "That God in all things may be glorified" (1 Peter 4:11) by—

1. successful and happy family life;
2. service within the church;
3. serious contribution to either literature or education.

As I looked carefully at the list, I realized that I would have opportunity to pursue any of the other goals at some other period in my life. But my time with little children is now. There would, I realized, be no repeat performance of these vital years. Wasted, they could not be restored. Used for other pursuit, they could never again be used for child nurture. I realized that how I used the time in these fleeting years (although they don't always feel especially fleeting while you're in them, I know!) would determine the sorts of values I passed on to my children, how much I helped them to develop to the fullest of their potential.

When a person realizes this, suddenly it becomes possible to set aside other aims, other goals—or at least make them secondary—and concentrate on the one important task for a few years. The number of years taken out for child nurture will be determined by the number of children borne and the time space between each birth. But the more a mother can treat this time period not as an interruption of her life but as perhaps the most important period of it, the greater will be her ability to cope with the stress of this time and derive pleasure from it.

It is ironic that just now, when the exceedingly critical nature of the early months and years—even the early hours— of a baby's life have been more thoroughly studied and reported upon than ever before, we should be facing the upsurge of forces driving mothers from their young. Years ago there was an old Jesuit saying, "Give me a child until he is seven, and you can have him for the rest of his life." It seemed a presumptuous statement, but it is now soundly backed up with research data. Dr. W. H. Worth, head of the Department of Elementary Education of the University of Alberta, summarizes the evidence "that the kinds of experiences that a child has in the early years determine his subsequent school career." His summary includes such statements as the following:

- As high as 80% of the shaping of the human mind takes place by age 8.
- The most rapid growth in many stable characteristics occurs in the early years.
- Variations in environment have greatest effect on a characteristic during its most rapid period of growth.
- Early learnings are difficult to alter or replace.[1]

The years when a child is basically entrusted to the care of his mother are the most plastic, most critical, most life-shaping years, not only in reference to his mental but also his spiritual and personal development.

Let's consider the pressure put on young mothers to look for some other method of caring for their children. Day-care centers are being demanded. Certainly they represent a need in our society as it now exists. And yet the very existence of such institutions is, in turn, demanding that mothers go back to work quickly. After all, the argument runs, is it fair for a mother to have to tie up her talents with just three or four children? Is it fair to herself? Fair to society as a whole? Furthermore, isn't it rather presumptuous on the part of a mother to consider herself fully qualified for the task? No doubt professionals trained in early childhood education would be able to give better training to the children, so isn't it in the best interests of the children themselves to place them under such care?

To all these lines of argument—on the behalf of the mother's rights to her own pursuits, society's rights to the mother's training, or the children's rights to professional care—the response is: "Nonsense."

By choosing to be a mother, a woman has temporarily laid aside some of her other involvements. She recognizes that bringing children into the world obligates her for their best possible care. The woman who cannot face making her

[1] W. H. Worth, "The Critical Years Hypothesis," mimeograph summary.

personal interest secondary to the concerns of a family just should not have children.

To the argument that the trained young woman owes her services to a wider society than the family, we need to reply that the very greatest contribution which can be made to society is that of stable, sound people for the next generation. All other contributions pale into insignificance compared with this. Today, most young women would like to make some contribution besides this one. Most of us would like to accomplish something for society—not only through our children—but also on our own. But we must set our priorities. Anything which would hinder our children from reaching their fullest development as individuals should be set aside during child-nurture years. "What shall it profit a mother if she shall gain fame and fortune, but lose her own family?"

To the argument that professionals are more skilled at parenthood than are natural mothers, the answer is clear. All of the training and skill in the world cannot replace the life-sustaining atmosphere which is created by love. And despite all that has been said about "over-mothering," I am certain that more children have suffered from the lack of a loving environment than from the love of their mothers.

I can never forget visiting in a home where a very fine professional nurse was baby-sitting for the infant son of a schoolteacher who had returned to the classroom within a few weeks of delivery. It was a perfect setup by all external criteria. Each woman was working in her area of speciality. Who could possibly suffer?

The child, that's who. The baby I saw that day was dutifully fed and professionally burped, but there were no loving syllables spoken, no mother-crooning, no whispers of "I love you, little one." Although physically the infant was being cared for meticulously, the self or psyche was being starved.

Something similar happens in professionally staffed day-care centers. Lots of skill, lots of know-how. But where is the love—that special love—not for children in general, but for one little child, "bone of my bones and flesh of my flesh"? That love which says to a child, "You are special. You are my own. You are loved for yourself . . . not for anything you do or do not do." A friend who is a psychiatrist commented to me recently, "I am very much concerned about the rise of day-care institutions. If identity is sometimes hard to achieve in the normal home with several siblings, what will it be for the child who finds himself surrounded by twenty or thirty other children?"

It seems to me that the estimation a woman places on her own abilities, her own personality and, above all, her own values, will in large measure determine her willingness to place her children under the care of a surrogate. The baby-sitters available, whether they be come-in sitters or professionals operating child-care centers or nursery schools, are often somewhat short of ideal. And surely the Christian woman will be insistent that her children not be left in the care of non-Christians. The wisest mothers simply say, "I have too much to offer my children to leave them with someone who has less to offer." And that "less" may be in any area: values, mental alertness, character training, firmness—or just plain love.

Another value which will be reflected in a mother's acceptance of a substitute will be the importance to her of her own relationship with her children. A mother who leaves her child from infancy with a baby-sitter cannot expect to be loved in the same way as a mother who nurtures her child in every way. Some of the child's love and affection will be diverted to the baby-sitter. Love *for* a child is something which comes as God's gift with the instant of motherhood. Love *from* that child is something which is earned by mothering.

Finally, the value which a woman places on the total personal, spiritual, mental, and physical development of her children will determine her willingness to let someone else take her role. Speaking in the context of sheep-herding, Jesus said, "He that is an hireling, and not the shepherd, whose own the sheep are not, seeth the wolf coming, and leaveth the sheep, and fleeth: and the wolf catcheth them, and scattereth the sheep. The hireling fleeth, because he is an hireling, and careth not for the sheep" (John 10:12-13). The hireling baby-sitter, whose own the children are not, cannot be expected to watch over their souls with the same eternal vigilance which characterizes the real mother.

During the preschool years, leaving children in the care of baby-sitters or a day-care center for any prolonged period of time should be done only because of financial necessity. I mean real necessity—not just a taste for more! The mother who is left by widowhood or divorce to raise her children may be forced back to work. Such a mother bears the extra responsibility of finding surrogate care for her children which will, in as many ways as possible, re-create the atmosphere of Christian love and individual attention which is found in the home.

Motherhood has always been a critical task. But we live in days which are perhaps more precarious than ever before. It is possible that some of the children we have borne or will bear will face a world entirely hostile to Jesus Christ. They may be taken from our homes into anti-God institutions; they may be taught by atheistic teachers to deny the God who made them. I thank God for every year He gives me with my little ones, determining to do everything in my power to lay a foundation of character, spiritual life, scriptural knowledge, and mental alertness which will stand them in good stead if they should find themselves in adverse circumstances when I am not able to help them.

Think of the reward which belongs to Daniel's mother. Before maturity, that boy hero of the Old Testament was torn from his family and country and set down in the pagan courts of Nebuchadnezzar. And there, despite all the enticement of prominence, prestige, and power, Daniel's home-taught devotion to God sustained him—even in the lion's den. These early childhood years are not years I wish to share with outsiders. They are years of planting. And she "that goeth forth and weepeth, bearing precious seed, shall doubtless come again with rejoicing, bringing ... [her] sheaves with ... [her]" (Psalm 126:6). I want to share in the harvest of godly and able and personally sound people who are my children, in the goodness of God.

10

Here a Little–There a Little

> Whom shall he teach knowledge? and whom shall he make to understand doctrine? them that are weaned from the milk, and drawn from the breasts. For precept must be upon precept, precept upon precept; line upon line, line upon line; here a little, and there a little (Isaiah 28:9-10).

HERE, IN OUTLINE FORM, is the psychologically sound method—God's method—for imparting knowledge even to little children. The longer I spend with preschoolers, the more I recognize just how perfect the method is. Maybe you have had the experience I have had, of taking a "crash course" in something. Summer school, perhaps. It's a perfect example of massed learning: material you learn in a lump. I was shocked after one summer school session when I earned honors in French and history to discover that a couple of months later I knew practically nothing about either subject. As opposed to massed learning, spaced learning takes place gradually, over a prolonged period of time, with intervals during which the knowledge can be really absorbed by the mind. Studies show that spaced learning is retained longer and used more effectively than massed learning. And it is spaced learning which a mother in the home is in a perfect position to facilitate for her children: here a little, there a little.

The mother who really wants to teach and enrich her children will not need to search out opportunity. She will simply need to be alert to their moments of teachability, those prized moments which come—a few minutes at a time, sometimes at widely spaced intervals—when the child is strongly motivated by some inner need to learn. Possibly a question has occurred to him. And he needs an answer—now. Or he faces a problem that is bigger than he is—and is ready to learn how to solve it.

Any schoolteacher who knows the tremendous effort which has to be put into motivating children for a learning experience in the curriculum, will recognize the head start which a mother in the home has. Here teaching does not have to fit a timetable. Instead, a flexible and resourceful adult finds herself juxtaposed with a highly acquisitive young mind. The exchange of ideas is automatic, continuous, and natural throughout the day. The mother's work in household routines is work which can be set aside; it does not have to move with the clock. And so she can be available for those little interruptions which constitute the perfect moments for teaching. Actually, the ideal opportunities for early childhood development are presented by the child himself. All the mother has to do is be aware of the child, responsive to his queries, and resourceful enough to lead the child beyond his initial interest to the wider world of knowledge.

In this chapter and the next, we will look rather carefully at several areas in which a mother who is creative and alert can strongly influence the development of her child. The wonderful verse, "Jesus increased in wisdom and stature, and in favour with God and man" (Luke 2:52) outlines the development of the whole child: mental development, physical development, social development, and spiritual development. These four areas of development—interlocking though of course they are—we will consider individually.

94

"He's not unintelligent," my mother would say, almost fiercely, about some child or another we were discussing. "He just hasn't been stimulated to use his mind." Or, "He's just not motivated to produce at school." I would smile tolerantly at such old-fashioned notions, with the secret superiority of an undergraduate who was taking the up-to-the-minute course in psychology. I just couldn't make her accept that intelligence was a hereditary thing. You either had it, or you didn't.

In the past few years, however, I have been interested to come across studies that show that Mother was, after all, right. While basic intelligence is indisputedly written in the genes, a very wide range of development of that intelligence can be affected by environment. Thus, two children with approximately the same inherited intelligence could perform very differently on the IQ scale, or in various learning tasks—depending on how that intelligence was nurtured during early years.

Whatever basic intelligence your children are born with, you will want to organize the home environment so that they can realize their maximum potential intelligence. As much as 80 percent of a child's measured intelligence at age seventeen has been developed by the age of eight.[1] So the years before the child goes to school are critical for mental development.

Creating an environment which both stimulates and facilitates learning need not be an expensive or an onerous task Any home which is rich in books which are read and enjoyed sets the stage for mental growth. Make use of your public library to keep a supply of fresh and interesting books available to your children. Use birthdays and Christmas gift times as an opportunity to give your children the

[1] W. H. Worth, "The Critical Years Hypothesis," mimeograph summary.

thrill of owning a book of their own. There is an abundance of material available from both Christian and secular publishing houses to help you encourage your children's innate delight in learning.[2]

Children who are surrounded with books, who are read to from a very early age, who are encouraged to turn the pages and talk about the pictures, will quite likely develop reading readiness at an early age. Play with the alphabet; words and sounds are a source of real delight to children. Little phonic rhymes are easy to think up: "What does B say?" I might ask my preschoolers at lunchtime (a favorite fun-teaching time). We say the sound together and then try to think up words that start with that sound. Then I quote their favorite "B" story: "A big black bug bit my big boy. Bang! That big black bug won't bite my big boy again." Simple and silly—but fun. All the basic phonic sounds can be taught in such a way, gradually associating letter shapes with their sounds. Even if you teach your children nothing further in reading readiness, you will have given them a good start.

I have taught each of my three older children to read when they showed signs of reading readiness (recognition of all letters of the alphabet in upper and lower case; ability to move eyes from left to right across the page; understanding of sequence in a story—and so on. I used a checklist in a reading textbook as a guide to their readiness). I studied two or three textbooks on the teaching of reading before attempting this, since my training was not in elementary education. I have learned a lot with teaching each one, but the biggest thing I have learned is how individually each child learns. It is this individual, unique approach to learning which the mother in the home can allow for. Even the best-

[2] I have reviewed the materials which we have found most helpful with our family in an article, "Mommy, Buy Me a Book," *Christian Life*, Oct. 1972, pp. 27ff.

trained teacher with a class of thirty or more six-year-olds must treat reading as a group-learning activity. Having had, myself, the advantage of being home-taught in reading—and the advantage throughout my education of being a fast and proficient reader—I have been anxious to give this advantage to my children. Besides, by teaching them at home, I have been able to teach from Bible readers and introduce the children to reading the Scriptures for themselves—before going to school.

Travel is another acknowledged mind-widener. If you can't afford to travel with your children on great world swings, you can take them for drives in "Magic Circles" near your home, exploring educational resources of all kinds with them. You can gradually increase the radius of the circle as the children grow older and travel becomes more enjoyable. Within easy driving reach of you, there are bound to be museums, historic sites, interesting geological formations, industries. Don't stiffen these trips up into educational tours, but do a bit of background reading so that you can answer at least some of the several thousand questions a family of small children can come up with when they see something new.

And don't be surprised if they fail to take in all that you offer. Friends of ours struggled with their family of three young children on a hot, sticky summer trip to the Alberta Badlands. When at last they arrived at the park, the children discovered swings and slides. Miles of fantastic hoodoos stretching below, even reconstructed dinosaurs, were infinitely less interesting to them than the playground equipment. But this does not mean that the children did not learn from the travel experience. For, however casually, they *saw* those badlands, and the visual image would remain to prompt interest in prehistory at a later date.

My parents did not take our family to any exotic places. But a semiannual visit to our grandmother who lived on the

West Coast was made as interesting and varied as possible. I can still remember the excitement of a brand-new notebook with my name and the title, "Something I Saw On My Trip" printed on the cover in my father's heavily slanted script. Each of us received one on the first day of a trip, and from those early records developed a habit of daily observation and note-making which is still a part of my life.

Even if you can't go for an extended trip or an occasional Magic Circle drive, you can still cycle, or go for a walk. Teach your children to observe, not merely to see. "Let's watch for all the signs of spring we can find today," suggested casually as you start off on a jaunt can make it mental as well as physical exercise.

Cheaper than traveling and almost as effective in giving children a background of experience and knowledge, is having well-traveled visitors in your home. There are no richer guests than missionaries, in terms of the wealth of information and interest they can bring to your young children's minds. Our children have studied world maps, looked with fascination at pictures in the *National Geographic*, and helped me look up material in the *World Book*—all because of a pending, or just past, visit from a missionary.

It's worth remembering, too, that there is recent evidence to indicate that aesthetics can promote the development of intelligence too. Children, researchers have discovered, do better schoolwork in pretty colored rooms. They respond to beauty: bright-colored wallpaper, pictures arranged on a bulletin board, a delicate mobile that moves with the breeze, a floral centerpiece. Simple tastefulness is within the reach of any woman. And knowing that it will actually stimulate her children's minds will make it even more desirable to produce a home environment that is colorful and attractive.

Another aspect of mental development is the stimulation of creativity. Again, a mother in the home is in a perfect position to do this. Creativity is bound—just as much as foolishness—in the heart of the child. Made in God's own image, all of us are creative. For He is the Creator. And He has made us like Himself. From the very beginning, children show flair for pretending, imagining, creating, which—if not stifled—can keep life exciting for them. When I see my little tots bubbling with ideas (my three- and four-year-olds engaged in spontaneous role play: "I'll be the mommy and you be the daddy"; or, "Let's play hospital. You be the patient"; or, "Mommy, there was an alligator in the bathtub, but we pushed him down the drain!"), my six-year-old cutting interesting shapes from colored paper to paste on her handmade Christmas cards, and my eight-year-old making a puppet theater from a couple of big cardboard cartons, I think sadly about the energy I used to expend in grade eleven and twelve classrooms, attempting to "stimulate creativity."

I find that little children need not so much stimulating as facilitating. Provide them with paper. Gobs of it. It doesn't have to be fancy—it can range from paper bags slit open and spread wide, to a roll of brown wrapping paper. They need scissors. Glue. Crayons. Felt-tipped markers. Paints and brushes, too, if you can stand the mess. And they need a few reasonable rules. "You may cut out of these old catalogs, but not out of magazines on the rack. When you glue, spread a piece of newspaper under your work." And away they go! You will find them giving you as many great ideas as you give them. And you can use any special occasion—a birthday coming, a relative sick in the hospital, Christmastime—to encourage them to make simple and attractive gifts, cards, and decorations. They will not only be learning to create, but to share their creativity in love.

If you are able to provide your children with the opportunity to take music lessons, you will be enriching their lives in yet another way. Don't wait until you are sure that your child has some special gift before giving him lessons. Almost any child can learn to play some musical instrument by the application of sheer perseverence. And that has to be on the part of the parents as well as the child. I was possibly the world's least grateful and least talented piano pupil. In a fast-moving, busy day, a half hour of practice used to seem like a yawning eternity. But my parents had their minds made up, and I had no choice but to take eight years of piano. I never became a great pianist, but few skills give me any more pleasure than the ability to sit down and play. I can't imagine my home without a piano.

Children cannot be expected to be long range enough in their thinking to recognize the value of music practice. It is something which, at least in the early, unrewarding years, needs to be maintained by parental fiat. Just as important, really, as the ultimate acquisition of skill in playing an instrument, with the pleasure that can bring, is the character development that comes from setting aside immediate distractions in favor of a long-term goal. Shinichi Suzuki, pioneer of early childhood music-training methods, has said, "Teaching music is not my main purpose. . . . I want to make good citizens. If a child hears fine music from the day of his birth, and learns to play it himself, he develops sensitivity, discipline and endurance. He gets a beautiful heart."[3]

It is a mother's privilege to teach her little ones that knowledge is at their fingertips, that you must simply "ask, and it shall be given you; seek, and ye shall find; knock, and it shall be opened unto you" (Matthew 7:7). I know of nothing as much fun or as exciting a challenge as stimulating young children to reach out, to learn, to create, and to express. The rewards are continuous, in a hundred little wonderful discoveries per day; and continuing, in children growing up with keenly inquisitive and acquisitive minds.

[3] Anthony M. Paul, "Music Is Child's Play for Professor Suzuki," *Reader's Digest*, Nov. 1973, pp. 156ff.

11

Tough but Gentle

SOME YEARS AGO at a church service in Alberta, Canada, I heard Dr. L. E. Maxwell, founder of the Prairie Bible Institute, tell of staying in the home of an old Swedish lady in Minnesota while on one of his many trips representing the school. He had a young family at home, and sighed as he told his hostess, "You know, I'm away from home so much that if my children turn out well, it will only be the grace of God."

The wise old lady replied firmly, "Mr. Maxvell, it vill *always* be the grace of God."

After we have done everything we know to assist the development of our children, we must always keep in mind that ultimately, if our children become mature, sound people, and disciples of Jesus Christ, it will not be because of us. "It vill alvays be the grace of God."

But God in His grace does allow us to be part of the shaping process. We have already looked at our responsibility to the mental development of our children. Jesus, you will remember, grew not only in wisdom but also in stature, and "in favour with God and man." He developed physically and socially—and it is to these aspects of child development which we now turn our attention.

101

The bodies of our children are given to us in trust, to care for and nurture until they are mature. Every mother knows the pressure of responsibility which this simple fact creates. And she knows, too, that children who are unhealthy will be unable to do their best in anything. And so a mother must watch over the physical development of her children as one who is answerable to God.

Preventive medicine in the form of sound and sane nutrition is probably more important than therapy. Supplying food for her family is something for which a mother is responsible day after day, and it is a means by which she can exercise a great influence over the well-being and productivity of her entire family. There is no need to turn into a food faddist; but when you consider the dismal results of recent nutrition studies in both the United States and Canada,[1] you realize that good nutrition does not come automatically or without careful thought and planning. The more I read about "additives and deletives" in on-the-shelf foodstuffs, the snugger I feel with a deep freeze full of home-grown vegetables.

Not everybody has the opportunity I have to grow and harvest a garden. (And believe me—I have no innate love of gardening. In fact, it took me several years of country living to get over hating it! Now I view it as one of the most worthwhile contributions I can make to good inexpensive nutrition for my family.) However, every mother can pay attention to nutrition. By reducing the number of "convenience foods"—prepackaged breakfast cereals, instant pota-

[1] Health and Welfare Canada, *Nutrition Canada National Survey Report* (Ottawa: Information Canada, 1973); and U.S. Department of Health, Education, and Welfare, *Preliminary Findings of the First Health and Nutrition Examination Survey, United States, 1971–1972* no. (HRA) 74–1219–1 (Rockville, Md.: DHEW Publication, Jan. 1974).

toes, TV dinners—she can both increase the nutritional value of meals and decrease their cost. Cooking fresh vegetables instead of opening a can; eating some vegetables raw; even—would you believe—brewing your own soups: each of these will be steps toward good nutrition.

If you have forgotten what you learned in school about vitamins and carbohydrates and proteins, write to your state or provincial Department of Health for the free material that is bountifully available to help homemakers. This material is likely to be soundly researched and presented in a balanced way that will keep you from falling prey to nutritional extremists.

Most nutritionists agree that breakfast is a key to good nutrition. If you are a breakfast-skipper, your children will want to be too. And remember, they won't be able to nibble their way through the morning the way you may be able to do. At the cost of self-discipline, you may need to force yourself to eat a sane breakfast. A pastor's wife once said to me, "My kids get their own breakfast." The kids were about ten and fourteen years old. "I have a friend," she went on, "who gets up at 7:00 A.M. to get her kids to school at 9:00! I'm not going to take two hours to get my children to school. In fact, most mornings I sleep in."

"What do the kids eat?" I asked.

"Not much. Tammy usually makes herself a piece of toast and has a glass of orange juice. Sometimes she skips the toast."

It was only a matter of minutes later in our conversation that this mother bemoaned, "Tammy just doesn't do well at school. She can't seem to concentrate." Didn't that mother know that a child who goes to school with an inadequate breakfast is a poor scholar—regardless of intelligence?[2] Nu-

2 Jane Stein, "How Good Nutrition Can Help Your Child," *Family Circle*, Sept. 1972, p. 34.

trition is the base point for performance. And what happens at breakfast may predestine the day for your child.

I'm no nurse, but my approach to home nursing is this: "Put yourself in the poor child's shoes." How do you like to be treated when you are sick? With tenderness and concern? Then pass it on. When a child is more whiny and grumpy than usual, don't try to spank out of him what he may need antibiotics to clear up. I don't own a thermometer—I've never been able to read one of those things. And I know we would be phoning the doctor twice as often if I knew the exact number of degrees of fever every time one of my four gets flushed. But I know the symptoms of fever and how to bring a high fever down. I keep a first-aid book handy. And I know when a child's illness has gone beyond my very limited medical knowledge.

Even when you have taken a child to the doctor, you cannot assume that the responsibility for his health is no longer yours. I have learned that you can't afford to turn your child over to anyone; you need to ask questions, find out *why*, and insist that treatment go beyond the symptoms to the cause.

As a family, we have survived all kinds of minor illnesses and injuries—and a few major ones. I find that health—or the lack of it—is very much a part of family living. The mother needs to learn and to communicate an attitude of optimism, trust, and gratitude "in sickness and in health."

Not all children are equally healthy. Some are prone to certain kinds of infection; others resist all the bugs. But all children benefit from an adequate budget of rest. How many times have you seen a pale, peaked child with red-rimmed eyes and dark circles, giving an animated retelling of the ten o'clock movie? He is the envy of his peers—that child with no set bedtime, the one his parents call "a real nighthawk." But he is being cheated of health and vigor.

104

Sleep patterns can be learned, and therefore can be taught. For the sake of both parents and children, firm and early bedtimes need to be set. Of course, a child's evening will be extended as he grows older. But well into his teens he needs a definite bedtime to protect his health. With firm and early training, bedtimes can be a pleasant part of the daily routine. We simply refuse to allow our children to fuss about being put to bed. And we are inflexible when we say, "Bedtime, Heather Ruth." We mean it—and she knows it. The result is children who waken rosy and rested—about a half hour before we're really ready to get up!

Family patterns of recreation can build good health and good habits too. The family that chooses vigorous outdoor recreation—swimming, tennis, skiing—and pursues it together is bound to be healthier (and probably closer knit and happier too) than the family that sits together in front of the TV night after night. As in every other kind of home-teaching, what you do will carry far more weight than what you say. If you want your children to be physically tough, built to endure—not merely survive—you will have to set a sound example for them, including exercise of some sort in your daily and weekly patterns.

By encouraging your children to learn recreational sports of the individual or small-group type, rather than depending on organized school and community league team sports for their exercise, you will give them interests and skills which will enrich their leisure hours throughout life.

The word "health" comes from the same Teutonic root as the word "holy." In our concern to help our children develop as *whole* people, we must not underestimate the importance of their being *hale* as well as *holy*. It is this kind of total well-being that Paul desired for the Christians at Thessalonica when he wrote, "And the very God of peace sanctify you wholly; and I pray God your whole spirit and

105

soul and body be preserved blameless unto the coming of our Lord Jesus Christ" (1 Thessalonians 5:23). This is a prayer we can well pray for our children.

How can we help our children develop into socially acceptable persons? How can we make them stable, reliable people? Once again, the Word of God gives us His methods.

Abraham was chosen by God to found the Jewish nation on the basis "that he will command his children and his household after him, and they shall keep the way of the LORD, to do justice and judgment" (Genesis 18:19). Commanding our children is essential if we are to know God's blessing on their lives and ours. Obedience is the responsibility of children to parents; insisting on obedience is the responsibility of parents to their children. And obedience training is the key to character and personality building. Only through obedience can a child benefit from the guidance of his parents. Children who are well and firmly disciplined in their early childhood need less discipline during adolescent years than do others. In the best interests of all concerned—parents and children—obedience must be taught in the home from the very earliest independent acts.

Even a seven- or eight-month-old crawler can be taught to obey a clear and simple "No-no." At first the word means nothing to him, but accompanied by a firm little slap on his inquiring hand, it soon takes on a strong negative value. I remember wondering if a child that age really could be taught to respect a word—until my own first child was crawling. With books on shelves within reach, I decided to teach Geoffrey not to pull them out onto the floor. It took only a very few slaps (and not vicious ones—just gently firm) to teach him to respect the word "No." And I will never forget the inquiring, questioning look he would turn

106

toward me when he would approach a "no-no." His eyes and expression said as clearly as any words, "Does Mummy always mean no? Or just sometimes?"

Consistency is highly important in establishing obedience. If you make up your mind that something is out of bounds, you must make it always out of bounds—or make the exceptions clear. A child is bewildered if today he can and tomorrow he can't. (However, rigid and inflexible consistency is probably not only undesirable but also impossible to maintain. There is nothing wrong with explaining that today they may not have a pots-and-pans band since you have a headache. Maybe tomorrow you can stand it. The consistency that matters is that your word always stands as immutable law.)

Good discipline actually teaches a child how to be reasonable, how to suit the action to the occasion, how to think about the effect of certain procedures. Of course this does not develop overnight, but it should be the long-term goal of firm, fair, and reasonable discipline.

On the road to this goal, it is wise to remember that the mother who limits the number of orders she gives saves herself emotional energy. Thus, when a child can be asked to do something rather than told to do something, a confrontation can be avoided. It's funny, though, how quickly the children differentiate between "should" and "must."

"Would you please put the dishes in the dishwasher?" I ask my older son pleasantly.

"Are you asking me or telling me?" comes his reply.

"I'm asking you right now, but if you don't do it, I'll be telling you!"

Nonetheless, even though "please" may represent only a velvet glove, it is well worth using in requests to children. Children can quickly learn that when Mother says "please"—they had better hustle.

The two years between one and three are crucial years in

107

obedience training. At this time, children can be trained to obey a parental command without exception. I have found that the best route is to give the command, allow an appropriate length of time for response, and then simply spank if compliance is not forthcoming. Of course, a mother can repeat the command once or twice, but the longer she waits before taking decisive corrective action, the longer the child will take to obey another time. Children are incredibly canny; they know just how long the tether is. If Mother first tells, then threatens, then pleads, then yells, and then spanks, the child will let her go through the whole routine every time. The mother who speaks, then spanks, shortens the whole routine leading to disciplined behavior. This makes life more pleasant both for her and the child.

Of course, discipline need not be administered in anger. Again: firm, fair, and reasonable are the key words. Yet it doesn't hurt children to see their parents angry when the child's behavior warrants it. Certainly our Father God reveals anger against unrighteousness, and children can learn to fear angering as well as hurting or disappointing their parents.

Many parents are timid about spanking. But I feel that it is the method of child correction that is endorsed by Scripture: "He that spareth his rod hateth his son: but he that loveth him chasteneth him betimes" (Proverbs 13:24). An even stronger passage links firm corporal punishment with ultimate salvation:

> Withhold not correction from the child: for if thou beatest him with the rod, he shall not die. Thou shalt beat him with the rod, and shalt deliver his soul from hell (Proverbs 23:13-14).

A firm leather spanking belt—not so narrow that it could cut—within easy reach, is a sound investment in happiness in the home. I am aware that that sounds like a contradiction in terms. But I know of nothing more miserable than an undisciplined child. He is pushing to find boundaries. When he does not reach them—or only reaches them after real naughtiness—he is bewildered. He is hurt and angry. The message which is communicated is that no one cares enough to curb him. He becomes resentful and does increasingly unpleasant things in order to force his parents to discipline him.

I have seen our house change from a chaos of whining, quarreling, unhappy children to a scene of purring happiness with the simple application of the spanking belt. And the change in scene has often reminded me of the verse: "Now no chastening for the present seemeth to be joyous, but grievous: nevertheless, afterward it yieldeth the peaceable fruit of righteousness" (Hebrews 12:11).

The Word of God also warns against overharshness (see Ephesians 6:4). Negative reinforcement (spanking) needs to be balanced with a generous program of positive reinforcement (praise, encouragement, expressions of pleasure and pride in the child). Both kinds of reinforcement are essential to child-training, but as the child grows older there should be an increasing proportion of positive over negative reinforcement. Thus, while a two-year-old may need a little spanking once or twice a day, a five-year-old will probably need one only once or twice a week, and a seven- or eight-year-old may rarely ever need to be dealt with corporally.

Because we hold the Christian view of the nature of man, we understand that our children have inherited a sinful nature along with the image of God. From the outset of life, they are in need of correction—both to make them well-behaved socially, and to reveal to them their own need of a Saviour. The correcting hand of a mother or father is the only place in society from which a child will receive discipline coupled with and stemming from love. In the school, the undisciplined and naughty, disruptive child will be disciplined. But it will be discipline meted out without love, and for the sake of the institution rather than for the sake of the child. Such a trauma should be spared our children by our own loving discipline.

Another element of social development is the instilling of habits of courtesy. Courtesy will spring from teaching the importance of other people, but nonetheless its outward forms must be diligently taught. "Hypocrisy," the free-thinker murmurs. "That's all good manners are: polished hypocrisy." I disagree. Courtesy and social manners are lubricants in the wheels of society which help to prevent friction. Jesus was one who spoke "gracious words." So, too, should be our children.

This came to me with a sudden jolt when a Sunday school teacher laughingly commented: "That daughter of yours can sure ask the questions!" I knew she could, but wondered just what she had asked.

Her teacher was a lovely middle-aged lady. "She asked me this morning, 'Do ladies have moustaches?' I told her, 'No.' So then she asked, 'Then how come you have one?' " Fortunately the lady had a good sense of humor and was able to laugh about it.

But I realized—a bit belatedly—that it was time to teach my three-year-old that it was impolite to make comments about other people's appearances. Politeness is really very simple: it is thinking about how the other person feels. And of course, this is something which needs to be taught to children in their egocentric universes. "Thank you" acknowledges someone of significance other than the child himself. So do "Please" and "Excuse me."

One more element of personal or social development we should touch on is the instilling of balanced feelings of pride in a specific cultural heritage, together with respect for all other cultural backgrounds. Your own acceptance of

110

a racial or ethnic heritage will be necessary to your children's acceptance of it.

Recognizing that God is God, and that He made you who you are and how you are, you should thank God for your own unique heritage, and pass it on to your children. Encourage your children to learn ethnic cooking and your other language. And at the same time, show them and teach them a deep respect for all other heritages as equally valid, equally worthy of retention and cultivation.

The way in which we raise our children will accurately reflect our values. If we really care about the kind of people they will become, we will handle them in a way that is tough but gentle. And we will hope that that is how they turn out: tough enough to take the strains of life, gentle enough to be truly humane.

12

His Best for Our Children

I HAVE A PRAYING MOTHER.

Two of my most clearly etched childhood memories relate to that fact. One picture is silvered with moonlight: it is a cold winter night as across the wind-polished pewter snowdrifts of a tiny Saskatchewan village, my mother trudges, pulling a sled. Her youngest child, just two, is bundled into the box on the sled; three other young children skip and run on ahead. With Dad away on business, Mother is on her way to prayer meeting, taking all of us with her.

The other picture is golden with afternoon sunshine. I have come home from school and called my usual, "Mother, I'm home!" Receiving no answer, I begin to search the house. And then I find her in her bright, sun-filled bedroom. On her knees. So absorbed is she in prayer that she has not heard me call. I stop, suddenly silent, on the threshold of the holiest of all.

And now I am a mother myself. And I am learning that being a mother drives me to prayer, forces me to reach out beyond my own resources, hour by hour. Prayer has become the very breath of life. Sometimes I find time to kneel and really articulate my requests, bringing them one by one before my Lord. At other times, prayer is a continuous—though often interrupted—conversation that I hold with God. It

112

starts with my waking words of gratitude and gladness, and goes on through the day as every problem and every delight is shared with my Lord.

At other times,

> Prayer is the soul's sincere desire,
> Uttered or unexpressed;
> The motion of a hidden fire
> That trembles in the breast.

J. Montgomery

I have often thought of the gem-studded breastplate that Aaron, the high priest, used to wear. On every precious stone was carved the name of one of the twelve tribes of Israel, "And Aaron shall bear the names of the children of Israel . . . upon his heart, when he goeth in unto the holy place, for a memorial before the LORD continually" (Exodus 28:29). This, I think, is something of the nature of a mother's prayers. Day by day and even moment by moment, she wears the names of her darling children close to her heart and brings them before the throne of God "for a memorial . . . continually."

At night, as I wait for sleep to slip up over my mind, I often have precious times of prayer. My mental image is that of bringing a jewel box into His presence and opening it lovingly, picking out the beautiful, sparkling pieces one at a time, and holding them up to His light. One by one I name my children and love them in His presence. And one by one I give them to Him all over again. It is a time that is sacred and sweet, a time of thanksgiving and praise, as well as of naming specific requests for each of my darlings.

What shall we ask when we pray for our children? There are the obvious things that come to mind. Their health, their mental alertness, their developing habits. We should pray, too, "Deliver them from temptation." And of course, we will pray in specific, believing faith, until each has made a clear confession of faith in Jesus Christ as Saviour. But if we stop there, we will have fallen short of what some mothers have claimed for their children.

We need to be spiritually ambitious for our children, not satisfied to have children who are nominal Christians, but longing to have our children enter into the fullest and deepest relationship with Jesus Christ.

In asking God's best for our children, we will never really know what all it is we are requesting. There are times when in motherly protectiveness we might draw back from asking God to mature and develop our children. It is at such times that "the Spirit also helpeth our infirmities: for we know not what we should pray for as we ought: but the Spirit itself maketh intercession for us . . ." (Romans 8:26).

In asking that our children might "seek those things which are above, where Christ sitteth on the right hand of God" (Colossians 3:1), we may be asking for them to have deprivation, hardship, and great testing—all in order that God might be able to give them His best and highest. If our children are to be "raised . . . up together, and made . . . sit together in heavenly places in Christ Jesus" (Ephesians 2:6), there is a precondition. Those who would know "the power of his resurrection" must also know "the fellowship of his sufferings" (Philippians 3:10).

I have a secret admiration for Salome, the "mother of Zebedee's children" who came to the Lord Jesus with the request: "Grant that these my two sons may sit, the one on thy right hand, and the other on the left, in thy kingdom" (Matthew 20:21). She is not generally held up as a good example. Her doctrine was all wrong, we are told. And so were her motives. But however that may be, she was ambitious for her sons—spiritually ambitious.

Jesus did not rebuke her for her request. He did not harangue her for son-centered motivation, nor chastise her for faulty doctrine. But He did warn, "Ye know not what ye ask." His reply underlines how serious a thing it is to be spiritually ambitious for our children.

Certainly Salome did not know all that she was asking. She was asking martyrdom for James; lonely exile for John. But she was also asking for them positions of responsibility and leadership in the early church and, through John's inspired writings, blessing to all succeeding generations of Christians. She was spiritually ambitious for those sons of hers. She was not satisfied until she had asked for them the highest place with Christ.

And I wonder—do we modern mothers dare to come with Salome and make such a request? "That my children may sit at Thy right hand." It is the kind of courage and ambition that we need.

Our prayer ministry on behalf of our children should begin from our earliest knowledge of their conception—or even before. Before we ever know whether the little one kicking up under our ribs is a boy or a girl, we can dedicate that life to God for His glory. And our prayer ministry will grow in scope and intensity as our children grow up. Even after our children have come of age, our prayer ministry will go on—holding our adult children before the Lord, praying His strength and His wisdom for them, claiming their children for God.

Cam and I have been doubly blessed in both having Christian parents. Often we have been unaware of the strength that their prayer ministry meant to us. But one long, hot summer a few years ago, when Cam was a political candidate in a provincial election, we knew we had drained all of our own resources and were still finding strength. It was then that we really became aware of the sustaining and keeping power which was being prayed for us by our parents. In that summer's campaign we faced every kind of temptation and every kind of discouragement. At the end of it, we tasted defeat (by just a few votes!)—a new and bitter experience for us. Yet, through it all we felt that "underneath . . . [were] the everlasting arms" (Deuteronomy 33:27). We became deeply grateful then, not only for our parents' good teaching and careful training, but even more for their continued prayers which saw us through to personal—if not political—victory.

Persevering, prevailing prayer, year in and year out, for each of our children, is both our labor and our rest. As I lay on the delivery table after the birth of our first child, I had a sudden, lucid awareness of one fact: "Now I'll never again know what it is to be free of care." That intuition has proven to be true, of course. But in prayer I am able to take that burden of care and concern and lay it before One who loves my children even more than I do myself, One who is able to do far more than I can do for them.

As Christian mothers who yearn for God's best for our children, we will couple fervent, prevailing prayer with patient, day-by-day teaching in order to help our children develop spiritually—"in favour with God."

SPIRITUAL DEVELOPMENT

"The only ambition I have for any of you," my mother used to say, "is that each of you will walk with God." What we would choose for careers, what further education we would take after high school—these were of far less importance to her than our inner, spiritual development.

Helping our children develop into spiritually aware and alive people is our greatest responsibility. Basic to it is value implantation—a process which can start when our infants are still tiny in our arms. Here are some of the values which I see as most important.

REVERENCE FOR GOD

Reverence for God is a primary value on which all other spiritual and religious experiences are based. "The fear of the LORD is the beginning of knowledge" (Proverbs 1:7). Reverence for God is taught by attitude: by your taking time—not just for a hasty grace before meals—but for true family worship; by your attendance at a church where the name of God is given the honor which is due; by your manner of speech with reference to God.

Knowledge of who God is, is of course basic. God should be spoken of reverently, lovingly, and often. I used to whisper some rhythmic lines to my little ones, something like this: "Who loves Heather Ruth? Daddy loves Heather Ruth, Mommy loves Heather Ruth. Cammie-Lou and Geoffrey love you, Heather Ruth. So do both Grandmas and Grandpas. But do you know who loves Heather Ruth most of all? God, your heavenly Father, loves you most of all."

Careless expressions which use the name of God should be avoided, since they will confuse the little child who is learning to be reverent and careful not only with the name "God," but with the Person whom it names.

LOVE FOR AND THANKFULNESS TO THE LORD JESUS CHRIST

At a very early age, children can be taught that Jesus is the Son of God. This is a seminal doctrine. The truth of it, and the reverberations of its meaning, affect all other Christian doctrines. It is the heart of the Christian faith. Christmas is a perfect time to teach the truth of the incarnation clearly and simply.

I used flannelgraph to tell the Christmas story, very simply, to my eldest child when he was twenty-two months old. And after I had told him the story a couple of times, he was able to tell the main incidents as I moved the figures on the board, answering my questions. "Who is the baby?"

117

"Jesus," Geoff was able to tell me.

"And who is Jesus?"

"Jesus is God's Son."

Rote learning? Of course. But a basic truth was thus firmly implanted.

As the calendar year moves along, Easter presents its perfect opportunity to explain the meaning of the death and resurrection of our Lord. Now the meaning of "sin" needs to be explained and understood by the child. "Sin is doing something wrong," I have told my little ones. And then I ask, "Have you ever done anything wrong?" I find that until the children are three, they shake their heads emphatically. But over the age of three, children are able to admit that they have done something (some very little thing, perhaps) wrong. Once there has been this acknowledgment, truth concerning the substitutionary nature of Christ's death can be presented.

"It was because of our sins that the Lord Jesus died on the cross. It hurt Him very much. But He died because He loved us. And do you know what? There's some good news, too. He didn't stay dead. He came back to life. And He is still alive. In fact, He is my very best Friend. I love Him for dying for me."

After such teaching sessions—often prompted by an Easter picture of the suffering Saviour, sometimes coupled with reading a few selected verses from the Bible—my little children have poured out their hearts in prayers of spontaneous worship and thanksgiving for the Lord Jesus' gift of Himself.

Long before they are able to enter into the mystery of the meaning of His death, though, children are able to understand, "We love Him because He first loved us." It is a truth which can be sung, rhymed, chanted, or clapped to. It should flow out of our own day-to-day experiences of love and worship shared with our children. We need to take the time to tell them the practical, little ways in which the Lord Jesus reveals His nearness to us each day. "You know what the Lord Jesus did for me today, kids? I was looking for my wallet and I just couldn't find it, so I asked Him to help me. And just a couple of seconds later—there it was!" The extent to which Jesus Christ is real and dominant in our lives will determine how real and ruling He becomes in theirs.

TRUST IN THE RELIABILITY AND RELEVANCE OF THE BIBLE

Trust in God's Word is another basic value which, once implanted in young minds, will be very hard for all the forces of evil to uproot. The authenticity and inspiration of Scripture has been affirmed by Christians down through the ages. Despite the attacks of higher criticism, today the historical accuracy of the Bible is attested by archeology as never before. If you yourself have questions regarding the unshakeable truth of God's Word, its historical accuracy, or the nature of its inspiration, you should take time to do some research to ground your own faith. Try Paul E. Little's *Know Why You Believe.*[1] Or, if you can take heavier material, F. F. Bruce's knowledgeable *The Books and the Parchments.*[2] Another real confidence-builder is *The Bible as History*[3] by Werner Keller. These are books to read for yourself so that you can share a reasonable, well-founded faith in the Word of God with your children.

I am convinced that if there is a rock for us to plant our children's feet on in the midst of the quagmire of relativism and subjectivism which characterizes much of both secular

---

[1] Paul E. Little, *Know Why You Believe*, rev. ed. (Downers Grove, Ill.: Inter-Varsity, 1968).

[2] F. F. Bruce, *The Books and the Parchments*, rev. ed. (Old Tappan, N.J.: Revell, 1967).

[3] Werner Keller, *The Bible as History*, trans. William Neil (New York: Morrow, 1956).

and religious thought today, that rock is the "word of God, which liveth and abideth for ever" (1 Peter 1:23).

The Bible should be taught inside and out. Children need to be given opportunity to get to know the Scriptures firsthand, not merely to be told about them. While Bible stories are fine and necessary for building general Bible knowledge, I am old-fashioned enough to feel that even young children can benefit from the Word itself—best read in a clear, modern translation. I believe that God's Word itself has power to speak as the voice of God to the individual mind and conscience. Long, long after we cease to have authority to guide our children's lives, the Word of God, carefully taught, read, and discussed with our children, will go on instructing them in their discipleship to the Lord Jesus Christ.[4]

Today, we compete for our children's time and attention from infancy. In our homes, television often takes up more of our children's waking hours than any other single pursuit. And let's face it: the values taught on television are not Christian values. They are the values of the world. The mother who is raising her children for God will keep a firm control on the "off" button of the television. And certainly she will restrain her own desire to watch television shows which could be damaging to her children. Anyone who shrugs—"They don't understand it anyway"—just does not know the learning power of preschool children. They do not merely learn what is taught; they absorb it: facts, values, attitudes, atmosphere, vocabulary.

As our children grow older, we compete for our children's time with the demands of school. And, like TV, we accept this institution as part of our children's lives which can be

[4] I have outlined in detail some methods for teaching the Scripture to young children in my article, "Program Your Children for Life," *Moody Monthly*, Nov. 1971, p. 75.

meaningful and valuable. But we dare not abdicate to television, or to school, or even to the church, the communication of the basic values which have been outlined above. For on these values can be built their own personal Christian commitment—the ultimate goal of Christian motherhood.

Living those values, firmly espousing and practicing them, will be the surest way to share them with our children. When these values are central in your life view, it will be only natural for them to figure large for your little ones. The "here a little—there a little" method is outlined in Deuteronomy in these words:

> And these words, which I command thee this day,
>   shall be in thine heart:
> And thou shalt teach them diligently unto thy children,
>   and shalt talk of them
>   when thou sittest in thine house,
>   and when thou walkest by the way,
>   and when thou liest down,
>   and when thou risest up
>
> Deuteronomy 6:6-7

Unnatural? Impossible? Not at all. If Jesus Christ pervades your life, He will be pervasive in what you teach and communicate to your children.

Once the values and basic truths have been thoroughly taught, a natural further step in the child's spiritual development is his own personal acceptance of Jesus as Saviour and Lord. And there is no joy to match a mother's when she hears her child say, "I'd like to ask Jesus to be my Saviour now," and hears him pray a prayer of saving faith. Spiritual motherhood doesn't stop there, of course. For the Christian mother realizes that childhood faith must mature with the child until it becomes a full and total commitment of the life of Christ in exchange for His wonderful life within.

God has created the woman as child-bearer. As Christian women, we will not view pregnancy as an imposition or an interruption—but rather as an invitation, in the goodness of God, to one of life's great creative undertakings.

I think of Carla. A defensive, fearful person, she was absolutely convinced that she did not want to have any children. "I have had it drilled into me since I was a child," she told me. " 'Don't have children,' my mother kept telling me. 'They're more trouble than they are worth.' " With such a heritage of unstated rejection, Carla was finding life difficult enough to cope with, without any children in the bargain. She managed to convince her husband, too, that children were a bad deal.

And then Carla met the Lord Jesus Christ. As she slowly opened her closed and frozen heart to the warmth of His love, something happened. At first she was puzzled by the new emotions that flowed through her, then almost alarmed. "I don't know what's the matter with me. Maybe I should see a psychiatrist. You know something? I feel as though I want a child!"

Later, she was able to analyze something of the radical change in herself. "Before I responded to the love of Christ, I just had nothing worth living for myself—let alone trying to pass on to another generation," she told me. "I was so locked up with fear and selfishness that I couldn't consider hazarding myself in such an adventure as parenthood. Now that I have learned to believe, I feel as though I could take the chance."

The love of God, the goodness of life lived with and for Him: these are the things that Christian women have for themselves and eagerly desire to share in procreation. As a maturing teenager, I looked forward to motherhood "some-day." I particularly remember one beautiful young bride

122

who used to visit our home with her handsome husband. They were recent immigrants to Canada. Everything about them—from their intriguing idiom to their restrained but obvious affection—fascinated me. They were both dedicated disciples of Jesus Christ, and the evenings when they joined our family were most often centered in discussions of spiritual matters. When Amy became pregnant, she became more beautiful than ever before to my eyes. The bloom on her cheeks the joy and anticipation that shone in her eyes, all spoke to me of the wonder and meaning of motherhood. She became my mental picture of "pregnant"—an ideal madonna figure to whom I could relate my own inarticulate dreams.

When at the age of twenty-three I became pregnant myself, I was grateful to God. The daily changes in my body were not something to repudiate or reject, but a source of wonder and excitement. I could hardly believe that I was really carrying a child—such an incredible gift.

Great expectations lead to the challenge of motherhood. To really succeed, we will have to combine the laughter of Sarah with the courage of Jochabed, the prayerful determination of Hannah with the submissiveness of Mary, and the faith of Lois with the thorough teaching of Eunice. And through it all—the weariness, the discouragement, the quiet joys, and the soaring sense of accomplishment—our hearts will sing: "My soul doth magnify the Lord, and my spirit hath rejoiced in God my Saviour. . . . For he that is mighty hath done to me great things; and holy is his name" (Luke 1:46-49).

Part 3

SERVE—and Be Free

13

"Keepers at Home"

"Maybe I shouldn't have bought it for her after all," Bud said, looking rather ruefully at the dishwasher he had bought for his wife. "Maybe if she'd had the dishes to do, she would have stayed home more," he said. "I still think a woman's place is in the kitchen." But Margo, his wife, had made for herself a wider place than that—and although Bud grumbled about it a bit, he was also proud of her accomplishments and glad to have her earnings.

Today's wife is almost bound to be somewhat schizophrenic about "her place"—battered as she is by the continuous announcement of a liberation she may or may not really want; knowing in herself that her greatest fulfillment will likely be found through her home and family, yet desiring to articulate her personality in some other theater as well. She flips the pages of a woman's magazine to find one page extolling the superwoman who successfully combines homemaking with an exciting and demanding career, the next page describing fantastic and exotic meals which only a woman with hours to spend in the kitchen could even begin to create.

To complicate things, her husband is likely to be a bit schizophrenic about her role too. Like Bud, he may think her place is in the kitchen—yet admire qualities which take her out of the home into a career.

Just what is "woman's place"? Does the Scripture throw light on it? I think it does, and I think it is possible for Christian women to find themselves standing in "an even place" if they will study themselves, their relationships, and the Word of God with care.

Writing to Titus, Paul outlined the role of young women: "... to love their husbands and their children, and to be sensible and clean minded, spending their time in their own homes, being kind and obedient to their husbands" (Titus 2:4-5, TLB). Writing to another pastor, Timothy, he advises that "the younger women marry, bear children, guide the house ..." (1 Timothy 5:14). In both passages, Paul argues that such behavior will best prevent any discredit being brought to the gospel.

Today, in a culture which offers many more options to women than did the society in which the early church existed (then, it seems, the only alternative to being "busy at home" was to be an idle busybody, gossiping from one house to the next), there is still a challenge to Christian women to "guide the house," to be "keepers at home." This no longer needs to be a full-time job throughout a woman's lifetime. Yet, this task has been largely entrusted to women, and that should be no cause for rebellion. For homemaking goes far beyond dusting and vacuuming and straightening and tidying. It has to do with relationships with people and with creating an atmosphere in which love can thrive. The home atmosphere, which is a creative combination of aesthetics, cleanliness, and personal concern, is a highly individual one. It is one of the most fruitful ways in which a woman can express her personality. And the ability to create a home—whether it be in a fine new house or a tiny basement apartment—seems to be instinctual to women.

We have a little cabin in the woods near our house where

128

short-term employees sometimes live. At various times we have had men employed in the farming operation bunking in it; at other times, girls who are working for me for a few months have made it a temporary home. When a man moves into the cabin, he puts his bag beside the bed and an alarm clock on the headboard. And that's about it for personalizing touches. But when a girl has the cabin for a home, she transforms it. Brenda lived there for only six weeks, but in that time she hung fluffy curtains, put down bright scatter mats, hung pictures on the wall, and covered the grubby sofa with a throw. Aileen changed the little house in her own way. She had little with which to add those extra touches, but nonetheless she washed and waxed and scrubbed what was there until the place shone with the glow of a home, despite its simplicity. These were single girls, but they were homemakers. And it was obvious that they had instincts different from the fellows who had lived there at other times.

I think most women—married or single—derive a great deal of pleasure and satisfaction from indulging their homemaking instinct. Each woman will express this urge individually. But essentially, homemaking will be a personal blend of aesthetics, cleanliness, and caring.

I have found real joy in discovering that in homemaking I share in the very nature of God in many ways. (Of course I reject the concept of God as somehow masculine. He's beyond that kind of distinction. He has let males share in some aspects of "His image," females in other aspects.) I think of the Lord Jesus saying tenderly, "I go to prepare a place for you" (John 14:2). He is homemaking for us— preparing an atmosphere where love can flourish eternally. Washing and cleaning are godlike functions. It is God the Holy Spirit who undertakes "the washing of regeneration" (Titus 3:5). Ironing and straightening, too, are acts which participate in the nature of God. I think of the Lord Jesus

129

Christ preparing a bride for Himself, "not having spot, or wrinkle, or any such thing" (Ephesians 5:27). As I make the necessary decisions regarding clothing for my family, whether I sew the togs or buy them, I am reminded of the One who robes us in His own righteousness, and someday will clothe us in "fine linen, clean and white" (Revelation 19:8). Meal-making, too, is something which is done by the Good Shepherd, who "preparest a table before me in the presence of mine enemies" (Psalm 23:5). And as I tidy and straighten the house, I recall that "God is not the author of confusion, but of peace" (1 Corinthians 14:33).

Because homemaking is essentially the demonstration of caring, it can be Christlike. He who "loved me, and gave himself for me" (Galatians 2:20) is able to help me love my family and give myself for them. Remembering that "even the Son of man came not to be ministered unto, but to minister" (Mark 10:45) helps me to accept my role of loving service with joy.

From such a perspective, keeping a house is not merely a chore; nor, on the other hand, is it merely a source of personal pride. It is an opportunity to share in God's caring for the human race. It is a way of saying to our family and to our friends, "I care about you enough to surround you with a tasteful, orderly atmosphere of love."

With homemaking, as with everything else in life, some priorities need to be established. Homemaking can become merely housekeeping if we don't keep a few things in their proper order.

CARING BEFORE CHARRING

Caring is the heart of the homemaker's attitude. While "maintaining" may be the theme of the housekeeper, "caring" and "creating" are the key words of the homemaker. In this caring, the homemaker realizes that children are more

130

important than tidiness. While she is aware of the need for basic order, she also senses the need of her little ones to play freely.

When Geoff was about a year old and beginning to really play with toys, I found myself wearing both of us out with many toy pickups in the course of the day. Now, with four children and a house without a playroom, I have learned to let the kids have the living room throughout the day. If company arrives, the children are trained for a quick pickup job. Otherwise, their blocks, trucks, dolls, and books are left undisturbed until just before supper. Then, "OK, kids. That's it. Let's get this room straightened up"—and eight quick hands go to work. In ten minutes the living room is ready for a quick vacuuming, tidied and neat for a pleasant evening after the children are in bed.

Caring is, of course, a two-way street. It is worthwhile to teach the family by attitude, action, and word, that since the home is a community of caring, all must demonstrate their care for the others by reasonable care and tidiness. Nobody needs to track into the house with dirty shoes on, but neither does Mother have to fuss and fume over an accidental spill.

The homemaker does not martyr herself by slavishly following around behind husband and children picking up their mess. Neither does she whine, "I think you could be a bit more considerate of me." She teaches her family that all need the help of each other to make the home a pleasant place.

PEOPLE BEFORE THINGS

While in the world at large our status may be measured by the depth of the shag in our living room, there has never been a measure of true homemaking that depended on

131

things. Jesus' warning, "Beware of covetousness" (Luke 12:15) was never more needed than right now.

This really hit me a year or so ago. I had made up my Christmas list: things I really felt I needed. And then I looked critically at that list and realized that most of the things I had listed as "needs" were items which hadn't even been invented ten years ago!

Missionary friends of ours showed slides of their work in Ethiopia, projected against our living room wall. "Here is one of our native pastors, ready to move to his new appointment out in the bush." The picture showed a smiling man with his wife and two children, each clutching a small package. "It's easy to move these men," the missionary commented. "They have so little to take." I sometimes wonder if maybe, when the Lord returns, it might be a bit hard to move some of us, weighted down as we are with "the care of this world, and the deceitfulness of riches" (Matthew 13:22).

We need to critically examine our own desires, the things we are pressing our husbands to provide, or the "needs" that are pushing us back to work ourselves. When things become more important than people, we have forgotten the words of our Lord:

> Therefore take no thought, saying, What shall we eat? or, . . . Wherewithal shall we be clothed? (For after all these things do the Gentiles seek:) for your heavenly Father knoweth that ye have need of all these things. But seek ye first the kingdom of God, and his righteousness; and all these things shall be added unto you (Matthew 6:31-33).

The woman who does a really worthwhile job of making "the little church" which is the Christian home a happy and harmonious one is, indeed, seeking and finding the kingdom of God in a very concrete way.

Creative homemaking is not a task which invites a ho-hum yawn of boredom. Nor should it conjure a picture of plodding on an endless treadmill. As Edith Schaeffer points out in *Hidden Art*,[1] no gift or talent is too great or too special or too professional to be given expression within the home. In homemaking we have the opportunity of displaying the image of God stamped upon us as women, as we carry out for Him and with Him the task of creating an environment where individuals can relax, where the frictions and care of the busy days at school and work can drop away.

Homemaking is a task which can be treated flexibly and individually to reflect our own personalities. Mrs. Whitman told me, "I never do anything just because it is a certain day of the week. How awfully routine! Washing on Monday because it's a Monday! Who says Monday has to be washday? I wake up and wonder what I feel like doing to-day—and that's what I do. That's what I call freedom—it's what makes staying at home interesting for me."

Mrs. Smith, on the other hand, has her work organized day by day. She follows her routine exactly—and quickly—and has extra hours each day to do what she likes. My own pattern (if a pattern is discernible at all) was suggested by a good friend over a cup of coffee. "After you get the school kids out, just tidy up the kitchen so you don't need to be embarrassed if someone drops in. Then you can pretty well do what you want until about 3:00. You have to work like mad, then, until the kids get home from school, but you can have everything in shipshape and be ready to start supper by the time they get in." Whatever plan works for you—that's the plan to use. Of course, if you are going out to work, you will need to be more organized yourself and also have the help of your family to keep housekeeping from being too oner-ous.

---

[1] Edith Schaeffer, *Hidden Art* (Wheaton, Ill.: Tyndale, 1973).

When you are a full-time homemaker, the day is yours. You can finish reading that fascinating book this morning, if you just put a bit of pressure on yourself this afternoon. Or you can put housekeeping on "hold" while you get a pet project done—then catch up later. A key to accomplishment was handed me one day in conversation with a mature friend of mine, a successful mother and now grandmother, who combines homemaking with a range of skills and abilities which are quite amazing. "My mother gave me the secret," Elsie told me. "She said, 'Never get out of bed in the morning without a definite project, something you plan to get done that day.'" When your children are babies, there are days when all you can plan is to get through the day—and that will be accomplishment enough. Later, you can include other projects in your days.

Homemaking does not insist that the woman's place be in the kitchen. It is also in the living room, the playroom, the study. "I'm sure glad my mom can type and write stories," Geoffrey told me the other day. "Not all moms are office moms." He was quite right. Some are kitchen moms or sewing-room moms. Some are moms who work out. But whatever kind of moms they are, they need to be first homemakers—keepers of the home.

14

Careers—for Whom?

BLONDE, BLUE-EYED Cheryl had been a good student when I taught her in high school. Not a prize-winner, perhaps, but a solid, careful worker. She completed her university entrance requirements in grade twelve. And then she married. A few weeks ago I met her in a department store. She was on her lunch break from her full-time job, clerking in a bank. "I'd rather not work," she said wistfully. "I like staying home with the kids. But you know how it is." She shrugged. We swapped news on various of her classmates. Then she told me, "I wanted to go to university for teacher training, you know. But he didn't want to wait that long, so I didn't go." She did not need to add what was obviously implied: "Now I wish I had taken my career training first and married later."

Chatting with Cheryl brought to mind my own near-miss on career preparation. After completing high school, I found a summer job in a printing establishment. The work was interesting. The pay check looked good. At the end of the summer, the owner dropped in to see me. "We like your work," he told me, "and I'd like to offer you management of the department you have been working in."

For an eighteen-year-old, the proposal was heady. A responsible job, interesting experience, good pay. What more could I want? A romance was flourishing, and marriage didn't look more than a couple of years away. I spent the next few days torn by indecision. If I were to spend the time earning instead of learning, I could buy furniture, help us get established quicker. Maybe we could even get married sooner! And then one day, I saw a glimpse of my lifetime goals and dreams shimmering through the haze of immediate distractions. All my life I had wanted to be a teacher—from before I ever went to school. If I settled now for something else, would I ever really be satisfied?

So I told my boss, "No thanks," and headed on to university. From the moment that my decision was made until now I have never had one moment of regret. I know that I would have felt—as my friend Cheryl does—cheated and disappointed if I had settled for a shorter route.

Who needs a career? Every young woman does—for a number of very important reasons: some personal, some financial.

(If you happen to be already married, with a family and no career—don't drop out. You may be able to develop a career later in life—we'll discuss that possibility in chapter 18. Meanwhile, this chapter is for girls who have not yet made their irrevocable choices.)

First of all, developing a career, taking time in your life for training, education, and experience, allows you the necessary time for maturation before you enter other complex roles. The process of maturing cannot be hurried. It takes nothing so much as time. And though maturity cannot be speeded up, it can be deepened and enriched by learning and living along the way. A mature woman with a wealth of background experience in education, training, and career will have more to offer in marriage than an immature woman. Or she may make, maturely, the decision not to marry at all. Either way, the development of her career will have stood her in good stead.

Shauna, a vivacious mother of two little children and wife of a young architect, commented to me, "Boy! It takes every bit of maturity I've got to cope with the demands of little children. I'm glad I didn't get started any sooner." Shauna had a university degree and several years of teaching tucked away before she entered her in-the-home phase—and didn't consider any of it lost time.

There is just no question that the experience and confidence gained in the practice of a chosen career will help you handle every situation in life. And having handled your own money will help you be a wise and appreciative manager of the money which your husband earns during your nonearning years. Bev, who had worked only a few months before her marriage, just couldn't seem to stretch Jim's earnings around their needs. She pushed him into taking a job he liked less but which earned more, but she still had the same problem. She had never discovered, by experimentation with her own earned money, just how much and how little can be done with a monthly pay check.

Since a woman who marries may spend many years of her life in a position of economic dependency, I think that it is psychologically sound for her to have a few years of independence and freedom moneywise. Perhaps she will want to build up basic investments to nurse along through her nonearning years, or savings for some of those special things which are hard to acquire in the early years of marriage. Developing a small investment portfolio is especially smart. It gives a gal an interest in the world of business as well as the pleasure of watching investments develop—both an outlet and an income during the closed-in years at home. A well-heeled friend of mine told me that the biggest mistake that young people make in regards to investing is to feel they have to have $3,000 to get started. "The best way to invest," she said, "is to start small. With a couple of hundred dollars, or even one, and a good broker. And go on from

137

there." Having just a little money to call her own, to spend or reinvest as she sees fit, may well help prevent a woman from feeling economic claustrophobia in the years after marriage.

For the career woman who does decide to marry and to leave her career for a period of time, there is another practical, long-term financial benefit from having chosen and pursued a career. Teaching certificate, nursing diploma, secretarial credentials, hairdressing diploma—you name it—if you've got it, it is a pretty comforting sort of life insurance. For me, the knowledge that, if something were to happen to Cam, I could support my family, has always been a source of considerable security. Not that it is the only insurance we carry, for we have always considered that the first choice would be for me to be able to remain at home until the children are all into school, at least. Nonetheless, my job credentials serve as an invaluable fallback in case of need. And I think it is common to young mothers to feel the need for this sort of security.

When Terri married, she went on teaching school for a couple of years and then welcomed their first baby. As far as Terri was concerned, she was settling down to have a family. But before the baby was a year old, Terri's handsome young husband was killed in an accident and Terri faced what every young mother fears: widowhood with a child to support. Because she had credentials and experience, Terri was able to find a part-time job in teaching. It didn't make her rich, but with what money she had been left, it was enough to let her maintain her little daughter and herself—and still have part of each day at home with her preschooler. It was the sort of exigency which any woman needs to be prepared for.

Of course, a career as life insurance is a two-edged sword. On one side, it is a weapon against insecurity, and ultimately against need. On the other side, it is constantly cutting into the consciousness of the woman: "You could go back to work, you know. Find a baby-sitter and go. Everybody's doing it." That wage-earning capability lying dormant is a continuous temptation until a decisive commitment is reached and maintained—to stay at home while you have preschool children, unless necessity forces you out.

In modern society, a married woman's whole life does not have to be bound up in the roles of wife and mother. If she has the desire and energy to pursue her career again, she can—perhaps after her children are in school, or later, in the "empty nest" phase of her marriage. A basic training in a career plus some experience in it will certainly ease that many-years-later reentry into the labor force.

Thus far we have looked pretty much at practical considerations: economic advantages in choosing and pursuing a career. But there are other values as well, which you might like to take into account before short-circuiting a vocational dream.

A career developed and pursued even for a few years allows a woman to discover her own deep interests and abilities. And while there may be a number of years in her life when she spends a good deal of her time doing things quite different from the activities of her vocation, it is good for her to know that she can succeed in a job. Furthermore, the intelligent choice and use of a career helps a woman to find herself: to discover at least some of her basic strengths and weaknesses, to ascertain some of her underlying goals. Self-knowledge is an important step toward full living and full giving of oneself.

Then, too, having a career is one of the best safeguards against leaping into marriage. Christian marriage is not a short-term affair; not an "if you don't like it—lump it" sort of deal. It's playing for keeps. And since the Christian woman accepts this, along with the scriptural attitude of submission to her husband, she is going to have to choose carefully, to marry a man whom she respects so highly and loves so deeply and cares for so tenderly that submission will be one of life's·great joys, not one of its heaviest crosses. The career woman who has assessed her aptitudes and acquired the training she needs for a career is in a good position to give careful consideration to the option of remaining single and living her own life. This option is discussed at greater length in the next chapter. For the moment the important point is that taking time in life for career preparation helps to postpone marriage until it can be considered maturely.

Here's something else about having a career before you marry. It provides a permanent window on the world—if you are sure to keep it open wide by reading and remaining aware of developments in your profession. It is pretty hard to keep entirely abreast of a field in which you are not immersed, but you can keep a professional interest burning. Cultivate a few friends who are active in your profession and who don't mind shoptalk; subscribe to a professional or trade journal in your field. I find it worthwhile to keep alive an interest outside of the four walls of home—it makes life just that much more interesting.

A final thought on the advantages of having a career: having pursued a career makes a woman an interesting and valuable partner for the man who is pursuing his. Even though his career may be in another field, she is able to understand something of the frustrations, concerns, preoccupations, and triumphs of a person who is practicing his profession or trade. Post-secondary training—in a Bible school, a college or university, or a technical training school—will put a cutting edge on your.mind and widen your horizons in a way which will make you a more equal partner with your husband.

The girl who has a career dream should certainly follow that dream. It will possibly mean postponing very early marriage, but that may well be all to the good. There is no reason why a girl should not take medical school, or law school, or business administration—if any of those are the things she really wants to do. If she is particularly good in mathematics, why not take engineering? If she wants to be a nurse and is able to handle the studies, she should not take the shortcut to nursing aide work in order to accommodate an anxious fiancé or pressing parents. If she wants to be a doctor, there is no good reason why she should be a nurse. On the other hand, if she really wants to nurse, she shouldn't train to be a doctor just to prove something.

Probably no pressure distorts career choices as much as "falling in love" during or before entering training. It is now quite possible to marry and continue training and career, but a girl should give very careful consideration, realistically and rationally, before curtailing or changing her plans to fit the desires of an eager young man. She needs to answer for herself these questions: If I make this decision now, will I be just as happy about it ten years from now? Twenty years from now? Will I thank my sweetheart for changing my life plans, or will I resent him for it?

Another thing which a girl needs to think about very level-headedly is that, in early marriage, she may be asked to sacrifice her career dreams in order to earn a living while her husband prepares for his life work. This can be a very costly sacrifice, and one which girls should not be too ready to make. Certainly, little could be said against a woman pursuing her career and thus earning while her husband studies. That may be both a way for her to gain experience in her own career and at the same time invest in better earning potential for her husband. On the other hand, the girl who settles for a minimum-preparation career so she can earn her husband's way through college, may be cheating both herself and her husband of a number of important things.

First of all, she may be cheating herself of a dream. There

are days and hours enough when the frustration of being the female partner in marriage builds up, without having any backlog of disappointment dammed up for additional pressure on a marriage.

Second, she may be cheating herself of her husband's respect and her own sense of equality. I remember Anna as a charming girl, with all the poise and grace of a fashion model. Through her high school years, she and Todd went around together off and on. When high school was over, nobody protested when Anna took a steno job while Todd proceeded to university. They were married. Several years later, with Todd the proud owner of a master's degree, Anna packed her bags and moved out. Why? Todd regarded her—and treated her—as his inferior, no longer fully equal. And although she had put him through university, he seemed to feel more scorn than gratitude.

Anna is just one of the innumerable young wives who have held jobs to finance their husbands' educations, only to discover that their husbands have outgrown them—or feel that they have—and the wives have to step aside. So laying aside career interest in order to please a man may be building difficulties into a marriage.

The choice of a career should be as big as the training school catalog. Each young woman will have to make her own choice, prayerfully, taking into consideration her own "bookish aptitude"—or ability to succeed with studies; her desire for further study; and her long-cherished vocational dreams.

Apart from offering opinions, her parents, friends, and boyfriends should stay out of this decision-making process. It is for each girl to make on her own, with God's help. The Lord knows what career or training will fit you best for the ministries He has for you. So learning His will is of utmost importance. He makes His will clear when your own aptitudes and abilities, your own interests and desires, the available opportunities, the counsel of older friends, and a quiet sense of inner direction all point in a given direction. When some of these elements do not agree with others, then careful, prayerful consideration will usually reveal the right course.

Sometimes God has His own special surprises. He did for my sister Margie. Margie knew what she wanted when she finished high school: a career in business. In fact, computer technology was the key with which she planned to open the future. In the back of her mind, she wondered if Bible school might not be a good choice too. She decided to let the Lord choose for her. "Lord," she prayed, "I am going to apply for computer training. If that is not Your first choice for me, just hold the door shut, please. If it is, let the door open, and I'll accept it as Your leading." She wrote a letter of application to a leading corporation, and then waited. And waited. Inexplicably, the weeks went by with not so much as an acknowledgment of her letter. At last Margie sat down and made application to Bible college. Her application was accepted, and she made plans to go. Only then—when her direction was firmly set—did she finally hear from the computer firm. The letter was most apologetic. Her application had been misplaced and had only lately been retrieved. Of course they would accept her as a trainee! But Margie only smiled. The Lord had gently held that door shut, and she walked confidently through the other, wide-open door.

As you approach a career choice, communicate clearly and openly with the Lord. As Elisabeth Elliott points out in her very helpful little manual on guidance, *A Slow and Certain Light*,[1] the most basic requisite to receiving guidance is willingness to obey. You must put yourself at God's disposal.

[1] Elisabeth Elliott, *A Slow and Certain Light* (Waco, Tex.: Word, 1973).

Then tell Him of your dreams, your uncertainties, your wishes, your financial handicaps. And then, knock on the door which seems right or best to you, asking God to keep it shut if He has something better for you. God can hold some doors shut and let others open and, by doing so, fulfill the deepest desires of your heart.

A sure and settled sense of peace is the hallmark of God's leading, whether it be into Bible training, a basic career, or higher education. Any of these will be an asset to you throughout life—married or single style.

15

"The Road Not Taken"

FOR SOME who are reading this book, marriage will be "the road not taken." You remember how Robert Frost put it:

> Two roads diverged in a wood, and I—
> I took the one less traveled by,
> And that has made all the difference.[1]

While this book has had a lot to say about marriage and motherhood, I recognize very definitely that there is a viable option to marriage—the option to stay single. That option may be ours through circumstances or by choice. But either way, if you're single: Congratulations!

Maybe you haven't considered being single something to be congratulated upon, but the congratulations come from no lesser a spokesman than Paul the apostle. "So then he that giveth . . . [his daughter] in marriage doeth well; but he that giveth her not in marriage doeth better" (1 Corinthians 7:38). As Terri Williams writes in an article in *Christianity Today*, "Marriage, as such, ought not to be a goal for the Christian. Marriage is proper and good, but it is not a

[1] Robert Frost, "The Road Not Taken," in *Complete Poems of Robert Frost* (New York: Holt, Rinehart & Winston, 1949). Used by permission.

goal."[2] Every young woman should have goals besides marriage; every young woman should seriously consider the possibility that she might be called to the single life. Going it alone is not for everybody, but neither is marriage. Jesus put it this way: "Some are born without the ability to marry, and some are disabled by men, and some refuse to marry for the sake of the Kingdom of Heaven. Let anyone who can, accept my statement" (Matthew 19:12, TLB). Jesus Himself chose celibacy. And hundreds of His followers, men and women alike, have seriously rejected the potential claims of family in favor of living an uncluttered life of service to Him.

First of all, being single must not be considered a blight. The best safeguard for happy and content single life is the personal assurance that you are a person enough to create happiness for yourself in either the circumstances of marriage or the circumstances of single life. The idea that marriage is God's will for every woman is as damaging within Christian circles as the idea that sexual activity is necessary to happiness is within secular circles. Both are nonscriptural concepts. Certainly everything I have said to this point reflects the high value I place on "the vocation wherewith . . . [I am] called" (Ephesians 4:1), that is, vocation to marriage and to motherhood. But nothing in this book—or anywhere else—should be construed to suggest that another vocation—that to single life—is not just as high a calling from God, or just as sure a calling.

No one could dispute that there are advantages to being single, and some of them are such that many married women secretly envy their single friends. There is the mater of personal freedom. Freedom to study. To work. To travel. Such personal freedom is unknown to even the most

<hr>

[2] Terri Williams, "The Forgotten Alternative in First Corinthians 7," *Christianity Today* 17, no. 17 (May 25, 1973): 8ff.

emancipated married woman, for even she knows that marriage depends upon the surrender, on the part of two people, of personal autonomy. Personal freedom is given up, first at the marriage altar, and then—even more utterly—on the delivery table.

This personal freedom gives the single woman the opportunity to pursue her career and service in an uninterrupted and undistracted way. Thus she has an equal footing with any man. She does not have to lay aside her career and then try to pick it up again. Her opportunity for advancement is thus far greater. She is able to give herself to her career in a way which is impossible for the married woman. "Single-minded" is a Bible term for uncluttered thinking. It makes sense in terms of the single person.

The single woman has opportunities to learn, to meditate, to think, to pray, and thus to grow as a person—all activities for which a married woman has to struggle to find time. Some of them the married woman finds well-nigh impossible to fit into her crowded schedule—a schedule on which her own interests and pursuits are placed at the bottom of the list, just after pet care. The single woman has many more hours of life to call her own, to use as she desires.

Financial freedom and independence are other aspects of single life which could be envied by married women. I realize that many single women do help support aging parents, or are considered a good touch for loans to "needy" married brothers and sisters. As I heard a single university professor once sigh: "If only my family would let me be single, I'd be well set up!" Nonetheless, the single woman can order her own resources toward her own goals without the pressing considerations of a family's priorities.

And, of course, there are the simple matters of being an independent, self-determining person, of not needing to submit in any of the basic ways we have discussed, and even, if it matters to you, of carrying your own name.

147

I am convinced that I could have been a happy single woman—partly because for me marriage was not a goal in life. I recommend to you the tone and attitude of such writers as Audrey Sands who declares herself *Single and Satisfied.*[3] But this does not mean that I am not aware of at least some of the problems facing single women. They have been voiced to me at various times by my single friends. I have a friend who recently completed her Ph.D. in English. And another who has traveled around the world, teaching in such places as Singapore, Italy, Canada, and now, Australia. And another who is doing post-doctoral work and writing educational textbooks. Such exciting people—with such exciting accomplishments. And it is from them, as well as from many other single friends, that I have learned what it is that hurts about being single.

There is the loneliness. "You know," an older single woman, a university professor, said, "I think what I miss most by not being married is not sex or even children—but just plain companionship, and the whetting of the mind that comes from the exchange of ideas with someone with whom you relate deeply." This loneliness is a constant strand in the tapestry of the life of the single woman. It can be combatted in part by cultivating meaningful friendships, by entertaining, and by going out. But the deep need of the heart for communion can ultimately be met only as the single woman communes with Jesus Christ in the very center of her being, and finds Him to be real and personal. Certainly the single Christian woman knows a sustaining companionship which the non-Christian woman could only dream of.

And there are the temptations to include sex in her life as a single woman. The sensitive, sane, and spiritual young woman will realize that not only is it unscriptural to engage

[3] Audrey Sands, *Single and Satisfied* (Wheaton, Ill.: Tyndale, n.d.).

in sexual activity outside of marriage; it is also damaging to her own person. In an article in *Vogue* (surely no conservative commentary), a doctor writes: "The interplay of sex and guilt is unending and the self-destructiveness of patients who suffer guilt as a result of some sexual transgression goes on and on."[4]

"Every other sin that a man commits is outside the body, but the immoral man sins against his own body." Paul states. And then he asks, "Do you not know that your body is a temple of the Holy Spirit who is in you?" (1 Corinthians 6:18-19, NASB). In the interests of the fullest and happiest life for herself, the Christian single woman will realize that the call to being single is a call to celibacy.

The "frustrated old maid" is a person of the past. Or perhaps she never did exist except as a figment of male imagination which found it intolerable to think that a woman could live quite happily without a man around the house. I am sure that some single women are indeed frustrated and disappointed, but probably this is not so much sexual frustration as the fact that their whole life view hinged on the idea that marriage was the highest good and that somehow they have "missed the boat." Actually, the single woman who finds her work satisfying and meaningful, who relates to others in a number of ways and gives of herself in service to the Lord Jesus Christ, will probably be no more frustrated—and perhaps not as much so—as the harrassed and child-worn mother who is her age-mate.

The deep instinct to motherhood is probably one of the hardest deprivations of single life. But this, like the instinct to mate, can doubtless be expressed in other meaningful ways. I think of our family doctor. He is not only competent and thorough, he is kind and even loving. He gives of him-

[4] Arnold A. Hutschnecker, "Do You Feel Guilty?" *Vogue*, July 1972, p. 99.

self to every family under his care. He puts us together as people, and sees us as whole people, belonging to each other in a family. He is a single man. It seems to me that he has made out of his practice a family which he can love. He has concern enough for all of us who depend on him—a rare man in a specialized and professionalized age. And I know that there are many single women who, as he does, give something extra in their profession or work. They give that something of themselves which the married woman has already given to her family.

I am convinced that an individual has only a limited emotional resource. Once that resource has been drawn to its limit (as it often is by a family), there is little left for anyone else. God sometimes sets very special people apart from the ordinary demands of married life because He needs to release their emotional resources for the good of a larger community. This fact came to me with particular force when I was in labor with my fourth child. Between contractions I read the biography of Henrietta C. Mears.[5] She was a woman whom God had set aside from the effort of physical motherhood so that she could travail in faith to give spiritual birth to hundreds of young people. She was a woman of such large talent that God could not let her confine herself to the love and demands of one little family.

Occasionally a single woman decides to share her life with an adoptive child or children. There is nothing wrong with this idea, although there are always complications in single parenthood which should be taken into account. Still, if a woman has a huge desire to be a mother, there is no reason why she should not adopt and love a family if she is able to carry the financial and emotional strain of such an arrangement.

[5] Ethel M. Baldwin and David V. Benson, *Henrietta Mears and How She Did It* (Glendale, Calif.: Regal, n.d.).

My single friends tell me one other problem which I wish did not exist—but which seems to. They tell me that they have real difficulty in feeling a part of the church, for they do not fit into its social structures. Unfortunately, our churches have become social institutions to a large extent. And, undeniably, that social structure focuses on the family unit. What about the single men and women of our congregations? How should the church minister to them? The best answer is simply—let's ask *them*. They are adults, and increasingly articulate about their needs. Single people must stop being treated with wordless pity by the church. Each church could well form a committee of single persons to meet with the pastor and discuss how they would like to serve, and how they need to be served.

On the other hand, single people can take initiatives in developing friendships with family people. The tired young mother with three children would probably more than welcome the invitation out to lunch. Single women need not sit passively by in the church and wish for something to happen to make them feel better. With a positive acceptance of themselves and of others—as people, rather than as "young marrieds" or "career girls"—they can help to develop relationships which will help to integrate married and single people in the life of the church. "There is neither male nor female" (and we might add, "married nor single")—"for ye are all one in Christ Jesus" (Galatians 3:28). This is a message which the single people of a church can help to communicate, by loving service breaking down walls of prejudice which may yet exist in some fellowships.

The happiest single women I know are those who are not trying to prove something, or even be something, but are simply living their lives for Jesus Christ in the most meaningful way they can find. Paraphrasing Paul in 1 Corinthians 7:20, 27, we hear a message that makes good sense to modern women:

151

Let every woman abide in the same calling wherein she was called. . . . Art thou bound unto a husband? seek not to be loosed. Art thou loosed from a husband? don't look for one.

It is the call of God recognized in our lives which makes the difference between disappointment and frustration on one hand, or fully taking advantage of the single life for His glory, on the other.

16

I Take Thee

ONE DAY when my mother and I were visiting, the names of a newly married couple came up. "Oh," I said, "I think Joan and Pete will probably be very happy."

"Maybe not very happy," my mother commented, "but probably as happy as most married couples ever are."

In her quiet way, she put her finger squarely on a popular misconception which I had echoed: the idea that marriage should be bliss, that the norm for human marriage is, as in the fairy tales, "they lived happily ever after." Actually, marriage is a very strange thing. Depending upon the people involved, it can be a little bit of heaven. Or a little bit of hell. Most marriages fall somewhere in between. Although marriage was designed to promote human happiness, many people find in it nothing but misery. Most people find some of each. Just what balance point a marriage strikes is based on two factors: first, the basic choice of a marriage partner; and second, the attitudes of both partners toward adjustment to each other.

Choices alter the flow of life irrevocably: no choice more than the choice of a marriage partner. Whom to marry and, indeed, whether or not to marry are two of the most important decisions ever made. Unfortunately, they are also decisions which are often made in an atmosphere of pressure and ardor which almost precludes rational, mature consideration.

The commitment to "love, honor, and obey" needs to be made maturely. It must be made with the understanding that it is a commitment which will supersede all other personal commitments, except that to Jesus Christ; that this commitment will preclude many other kinds of possible personal commitment; and, perhaps most important, that it is a commitment for life. Any commitment short of this is less than a true marriage pledge. I wonder how many couples, legally married within a church, are actually living in adultery because their commitment to each other is less than total. Only in total life commitment can two become one; only as two become one is marriage really effected.

Such a commitment calls for careful preparation of mind. This is, basically, the purpose of a courtship and engagement period before marriage. Now, this purpose is often obscured in the heat of "being in love." Our society has put so much emphasis on the physical aspects of male-female relationships that sometimes even Christian young people forget that there are many other facets to a worthwhile relationship.

Many kinds of marital problems can actually be presolved if a couple uses the period between initial love and consummation in marriage wisely and well. Perhaps this is one of the practical reasons why God's Word rules out sexual activity before marriage. The engagement waiting time, if observed in chastity, provides a crucible in which ideas and expectations can be brought to the boil. Really working through differences can be far better achieved by two people for whom sexuality is an unresolved tension, than for those to whom it is an exciting game. When a couple allow themselves sexual privileges premaritally, they actually short-circuit the necessary development of growing together, sorting out their individual aims and ideals.

Engagement is a solemn promise, publicly expressed, and

often sealed by a prized piece of jewelry—the diamond ring. Once this preliminary commitment has been made, flirting days are over. Alternative mates are permanently discarded as the couple narrows its attention and affection to each other. This period of separation from other potential mates is a prelude to lifetime fidelity, and with it comes the security in which serious preparations can be made.

This is a time for personal preparations: adjustments to each other's preferences and interests; facing up to the chosen partner as he really is. In the engagement period, the masks of courtship—at least to some extent—should be laid aside. "Every engaged fellow should see his fiancée in hair curlers, cold cream and housecoat at least once," I remember a minister saying. "And the girl should have the privilege of seeing her beloved's face unshaven." (Or, in some cases, shaven. A handsome, bearded brute may actually have no chin at all. Worth knowing beforehand!)

Now is the time for some honest questions and answers. What, really, is the prospective groom looking for in a wife? Are you that person? And if not, is he able to set aside some of his expectations in favor of the person you are? How much will you be able to adjust to meet his ideals without denying your basic identity? The more honestly a couple gets to know each other during engagement, the less jolting will be the thud when the honeymoon is over.

When you were a little girl, you probably had some sort of romantic notion about whom you would marry. I always fantasized housekeeping with a tall, blond, blue-eyed man. The man I married is short, black-haired, and green-eyed. But those visual expectations were of minor importance compared with more basic expectations. Are you the kind of woman who looks forward to being provided for? You will need to be sure that he understands and is capable of fulfilling that ideal. Or are you the kind of woman who has every intention of pursuing a career together with marriage?

155

Then be sure he understands and is able to cope with that.

Of course, you cannot foresee every marriage difficulty. But you can come to some basic agreement on basic issues. Do you both want children in your marriage? Soon, or later on? Is he willing to support you if you do bear children? If he expects you to go out to work, is he willing to pitch in and help with the housework? What are his expectations concerning housewifery? Can *you* bake that cherry pie he always dreams of—or is he able to forget his dream and not feel cheated?

Work these problems through carefully. Talk them through. That's what an engagement period is all about. If you can work out these basics in that atmosphere of sexual tension which will characterize a nonconsummated relationship, there is every chance that you will be able to build a happy marriage once you are able to enjoy sex in all its healing capacity.

If you really want to know the joys of mutual submission, voluntary submission, and love in your marriage, you need to assess very carefully whether or not the man who invites you into marriage is one who will submit to you, one to whom you can submit, and one who has enduring qualities on which love can thrive. There is just no way that a woman who cares about her own happiness and that of her future husband and even more future family, will make such a decision without prayerful consideration. Besides a general feeling of love, she will need to consider other important factors.

Is the prospective husband a believer?

"She is at liberty to be married to whom she will; only in the Lord" (1 Corinthians 7:39). That's the way Paul sets the parameters of free choice of a marriage partner. The Christian woman who marries an unbeliever in disobedience to the Word of God is inviting a life of heartache. No amount of rationalizing can explain away clear directives from God's Word (see also 2 Corinthians 6:14-18). The hope of bringing your mate to Christ after marriage is a dim one; ask the woman who married with that hope.

IS HIS DEDICATION TO CHRIST EQUAL TO YOURS?

My parents often said, "It's not enough just to marry a Christian. Be sure you marry a dedicated Christian." Many women have had their lives "bound in the shallows" because of marrying men who, though believers, are half-hearted in their commitment to Jesus Christ.

DO YOU HAVE MUTUAL LIFE AIMS?

If your aims are divergent, you will be frustrated throughout life. If your aims are for continuing education and travel, for instance, and his are to establish a business, you will have to work out beforehand how the two aims can jibe without undue sacrifice on either part. As another illustration: if you feel you would like to live a simple life in full-time Christian service and his desires are for immediate financial security (or *vice versa*), perhaps you had better part.

DO YOU SHARE SOME MUTUAL INTERESTS?

Or, at the very least, do you respect each other's interests? There is no need for two people to have identical interests in order that a marriage function well. In fact, interests can be widely divergent as long as there is mutual respect for each other's interests—and encouragement by each partner to pursue individual interests. But it can get lonely going to symphonies alone, and your husband may really want you to go camping with him. It is well to remember that the very heart of marriage is companionship, so things in which two can share an interest are a positive advantage.

DO YOU RESPECT THE MAN?

I mean *really*. Do you think of him as intelligent, rational, resourceful? Is he able to handle money with competence? Does he succeed at some of the things which are important to you? If you don't respect him now, you may find that a fond feeling for a blockhead is not quite a deep enough emotion on which to build a lifetime of respect and submission.

And if the man you think you love doesn't measure up—what then? Or if you haven't found a man with these qualities—what? The answer is obvious to me: stay single. There are lots worse things than being single. And until you find a man with qualities big enough for you to really "love, honor, and obey" him, you are a lot better off hanging onto your independence.

At the same time, it is probably well to remember that there are no perfect people, that even in the very best and happiest of marriages there is no such thing as complete bliss. I recall hearing Theodore Epp say, "Since the fall, every rose has had its thorn." Certainly it is true of the rose which is marriage. At its best, marriage is a matter of two imperfect people loving each other as they are.

I shall never forget one bleak night when Cam and I had been married a little more than a year. I lay in bed beside my husband, suddenly aware that marriage was not all that I had expected. Cam sensed something wrong. "What is it?" he coaxed.

I started to verbalize the things that had built up inside of me. The romance seemed to have gone out of life; he didn't open the car door for me always; I hadn't had a flower since my wedding day; he didn't seem to court me anymore— My list went on and on.

And when I was all finished, there was a long silence in the darkness. And then my husband spoke. I was rigid, braced for his list of countercharges. And what he said was, "I'm sorry, darling. For my part, I'm completely satisfied."

I was overwhelmed. Completely satisfied—with me! Without apple pies or mended socks—or even dusted corners. With a wife who was never quite caught up with all the things she had on the go.

In that moment I understood how good and real our marriage was, how trivial the little things I had let become big in my mind. Suddenly I realized that Cam knew what I was just groping toward: that marriage is not perfection, but compromise. Not bliss, but a happy acceptance of each other.

It is to this kind of union that a bride can look forward when, having carefully assessed her decision, she makes a clear-eyed commitment: "I take thee—for better or for worse."

17

From Career Girl to Housewife

I STARTED OUT in marriage as a "career wife." The first three years of our marriage were happily hectic as my husband and I shared earning responsibilities and household chores. We taught school together, went to university together, washed floors and did dishes together. It was great fun! But from the first I knew that this would be only an interim arrangement. Together, we looked forward to the time when we would become a family.

Then came my first pregnancy and a great shift in roles. From career wife to housewife was quite a change, and that first year at home brought me moments of deep depression. There was a sudden closing in of my horizons, a growing realization that while Cam would go out each morning to pursue his career, I would stay in day after day. And as my husband shouldered the full earning responsibility, I found myself not only washing but also wiping the dishes. It was fair enough, I realized, but not entirely fun.

Of course, I was not the only young wife to find coping with my new role somewhat difficult. I have found that most young career women have experienced some degree of depression and disorientation in the adjustment process. One young mother told me, "The week I quit work, it suddenly hit me. I was utterly dependent!"

The problem of taking on a role of "utter dependence" is

one which we have already looked at in chapter 6. However, learning to live with it is probably the really big jolt that comes to the career girl when she leaves behind her job to become a full-time housewife. And this dependency, she gradually learns, is not only financial; it is also social and emotional. Because of this, the change from career girl to homemaker puts a strain on a young wife—and on a young marriage too. Yet the difficulties can be lessened at least a bit if they are understood, and prepared for.

The wife's financial dependency necessitates adjustment on the part of both husband and wife. However they may have handled finances while both were working, a couple must now work out a way in which one income can be handled to the satisfaction of two people. Some couples see this problem ahead and soften the adjustment by using the wife's earnings strictly for savings, securities, or capital purchases and living on the husband's earnings from the beginning.

When the amount of money coming in is suddenly less and the demands on it are suddenly greater, there are bound to be misunderstandings if great care is not taken to keep communications open. Because a young man may be a bit unsure about the adequacy of his income, nervous and insecure in his new role as a supporter, a wife may need to summon more than the usual amount of tact and grace to set the scene for free and clear-headed discussion.

The best time for this is prior to the wife's quitting work. A careful accounting of household costs for a period of a few months before she quits will allow her to estimate how much she will need to meet grocery, clothing, and personal expenses. The reading and discussing of such a book as George M. Bowman's *How to Succeed with Your Money*[1] can form the basis for budget talk that makes sense.

[1] George M. Bowman, *How to Succeed with Your Money*, rev. ed. (Chicago: Moody, 1975).

Although the financial adjustment may be a bit ticklish, it is an obvious one, and most husbands can be made aware that the newly dependent wife has the need of a household operating allowance, or access to a joint checking account. However, she may have other needs which are more difficult to communicate to her husband—or even to analyze for herself. As long as she was working away from home every day, she had a group of adult peers who provided her with social and intellectual stimulation. Now she depends upon her husband for such an ordinary thing as conversation. However endearing the baby's babble may be, it does not satisfy the need of a woman for discussion and the interplay of ideas.

I remember struggling to pinpoint what was wrong with me several months after our firstborn had arrived. I knew I should be all done with after-baby blues, but I was bluer than ever. Gradually I realized that I was lonely. Bitterly lonely. Cam was holding his school principalship and farming on the side. I had days and evenings to myself. When at last I knew what my problem was, I told Cam about it. He was startled. "You have the baby!" he reminded me.

"And he provides about as much companionship as a puppy," I blurted.

After that, Cam and I worked consciously to find ways in which we could share more time together, and ways in which to make the time we did have more meaningful. But many young women will find, as I did, that the wife may have to take the initiative in expressing her need of friendship and companionship. Before the baby arrives, a carefully prepared supper can be lingered over for conversation. But candlelight and silver are much easier to idealize than to realize when baby has a 6:00 P.M. feeding—and is there a baby who doesn't? So a practical arrangement is to allow for suppertime and baby's feeding, and then give husband and offspring time to romp while you do the clean-up chores

162

in the kitchen. Hopefully, you might even get your hair combed and your face freshened up.

When the baby is tucked away, you can be ready to sit down in the quiet living room with a starter question or idea. "Well, what happened at work today?" may net you only a grunt. But, "Heard any reactions to the Mid-East crisis? I read in *U.S. NEWS* that—" might provoke a bit more interest. Just be sure to lose the TV schedule before you make this attempt, or you may be drowned out just when conversation was about to happen.

Another way to capitalize on your husband's companionship is to have friends over—friends you know he enjoys as much as you do. In the tiredness of prenatal or post-childbirth days, entertaining can be pretty taxing; keep the evening simple and intimate. Just another couple in for coffee and dessert is probably easier on your frayed nerves than a crowd. And you will probably get in on some good, interesting conversation—provided you chose interesting people to invite.

A fact that is hard to realize is that your husband, going out to work every day, seeing new faces and meeting new ideas, feels little need for an evening out. At least, my husband never did. At first I resented this. "He never thinks of how I don't get out of this house for days on end." Martyrdom was about to set in when it finally occurred to me that I was expecting too much. I was expecting my husband to know my mind and to feel my eagerness for a chance to get out and do something different. I gave up on that angle and instead took the initiative. "Darling, there's a concert at the auditorium on Wednesday night. Shall I get a sitter?" It worked; and, when I want a night out badly enough, I know how to get it.

One of my hardest adjustments was to what I call "the discipline of weakness." I didn't just bounce back to vigorous good health within a few weeks or even months after

163

childbirth. In fact, from the time I began having children until a couple of years after the last one was born, I really didn't know what it was like to feel well. I learned to walk carefully on ice, not to climb up ladders, to take morning and afternoon naps—all for the sake of the unnamed, unknown child I was carrying within. And after the babies were born, I learned other precautions: not to get a chill, not to invite in too many guests for fear of suddenly collapsing into tears, and still to take afternoon naps. I forgot what it was like to run, to jump, to toboggan—and wondered vaguely what it would be like to have energy for such frivolity. In those days I came to realize how great and kind God's plan for families really was. I could give Cam a tender kiss and watch him go out to work, then lie down again for a while and rest.

Now, with health and strength returning (Mitchell, my youngest, will be three next week!), I am rediscovering the joys of vitality. But the discipline of weakness has changed me. It has, at least, made me appreciative of my husband's strength and grateful for whatever strength the Lord allows me to use.

A dedicated homemaker once told me, "When my children were young, I disciplined myself not to read books so that I could get my work done." I have decided on just the opposite: I discipline myself to keep reading. It is important to me, for I do not want to let my mind become sterile and dry from the lack of the nourishment of new ideas, and the exercise of grappling with real issues. Increasingly, as my family grows older, they will need to know me not only as a loving and prayerful mother, but also as one who is mentally alert and flexible. In an age when young people learn early to respect intelligence above most other values, it seems to me to be a good idea to keep well-informed and mentally active.

I have learned—as have many other professional women—

that it is easier to stay in the home if I have some outlet for my own professional interests. I know women who nurse one day a week; some who teach music lessons in their homes; some who tutor several pupils. I write. And I think that whatever outlet you need to keep from feeling "dried up" or "out of touch" is valuable to your whole family, so long as priorities are kept clearly in mind.

The answers to adjusting to an indeterminate suspension, or perhaps termination, of a career are not easily found. But the woman who has chosen marriage and then has chosen to bear children will want to be sure that the answers she finds are both scriptural and sane.

The ideal woman of Proverbs 31 represents a mature woman, one who has found a balance point between personal interests and family demands, and manages them with a minimum of conflict. She is a woman who is vigorous and alert—vitally concerned with the management of her household but also interested in a home-based business of her own (v.24), in making wise investments (v.16), in her personal health and appearance (v.22). Here is a woman who makes a career of her family without slipping into martyrdom over it. Small wonder that "her children arise up, and call her blessed; her husband also, and he praiseth her" (Proverbs 31:28).

As a teacher retired to the kitchen, I know how taxing the adjustment from career to home can be. And I find that it is an adjustment which one goes on making—with changes to be made as each additional child joins the family, or as a husband changes jobs. But I have found that for a woman whose interests lie in matters intellectual and spiritual, the home is an ideal place to go on growing. Boredom—of which we read so much—has never been the slightest problem to me. Organizing to accommodate all my interests is a far greater one. With discipline, it is possible to go on reading, thinking, developing—and homemaking.

165

I can't say that I made the adjustment from career wife to housewife terribly gracefully or with hydraulic smoothness. But I managed to make it; and the opportunities I have at home, both for myself and for my family, are some I would be very sorry to have missed.

18

And Back Again

DAWN HAD NURSED for only a few months after graduation from training when she and Maurice were married. Babies were next on the schedule. And then—at last—the children were in school, and Dawn got back into whites.

She had not been working many weeks when one afternoon, as she struggled from her daytime sleep to answer the jangling telephone, she fell on the stairs and broke an ankle. It was a compound fracture, and Dawn found herself grounded at home again. "The Lord knew that I was just in too big a hurry to get back to work," she told me. "He just brought everything to a halt. And now that I'm back at home, I have found out just how much Maurice and the kids need me there. For a while longer, anyhow."

Several years later, when the ankle had healed and the kids were further along in school, Dawn took a job again. She was able to get a steady day shift—one that meant she was home every day when the children got off the bus. Everything was working beautifully.

And then, one day, I saw her limping painfully, her ankle taped again. "Oh no!" I gasped. "What happened?"

Dawn explained how she had twisted her ankle, aggravating the old injury. "The Lord caught up to me, Maxine," she said. "I went back to work, you know, and He just doesn't let me get away with it. Others seem to be able to—but not me!"

Deciding when and how and if to go back to work is a problem which confronts all married women of our generation. The pressure of public opinion is in favor of a return to the labor force; the cost of living makes it a very attractive option. Yet, we do have a God who recognizes individual differences, despite a society that fails to understand them. The same pressure of public disapproval that once held unhappy and frustrated women in the home indefinitely may now force reluctant, home-loving women back out to work. As the mature Christian woman considers the options which reopen to her as her children enter school, she needs to be prayerful and open to the leading of the Lord. She needs to remind herself that true freedom is the freedom to choose. And she listens to Paul's warning, "Don't let the world around you squeeze you into its own mold, but let God remold your minds from within, so that you may prove in practice that the plan of God for you is good" (Romans 12:2-3, Phillips).

In considering reentry into a career, the married woman will assert her freedom in Christ by assessing her own interests and goals, the interests of her family, and the claims of Jesus Christ. As much as possible, she will make her decision based on her own unique circumstances rather than on the pressures of society.

There are many questions which need to be answered. They are questions which we, as individuals, need to answer for ourselves. "How strong am I?" is one of the most important of these questions. The women who issue the strident summons back to work must be physically strong women. But not all of us are so blessed. If a woman is not exceptionally healthy and strong, the stress of a job plus homemaking may well be sufficient to bring her to a real breakdown. I have seen so many tired, haggard-looking women in jobs from store-clerking to nursing that I have had to raise the question to myself.

Not long ago, as I walked carefreely down a school hall after having delivered a birthday present to my party-bound son, a married woman teacher looked at me enviously. "You lucky girl," she said. "Just staying home. What a life! Wouldn't we all love to lead it." When I think about hurrying back to take a job in a couple years' time, I remember her white, tired face and red-rimmed eyes and envious tone—and think again.

Health is a gift from God; it should not be squandered. And our ability to minister to the needs of our husbands and families—as well as to perform adequately on a job—is very dependent on our measure of health. In a valuable little book, *Women and Fatigue*, Dr. Marion Hilliard points out:

> Probably the mother of a family of small children is the most likely of all women in today's society to suffer [from fatigue]. The wife who tries to manage a home and also go out to work is a close runner-up.[1]

This woman doctor goes on to say,

> The fatigue of a mother is the single most important element in any family's emotional well-being. If the mother is too tired, she can't be judicious in the treatment and discipline of her children, or give the proper love and attention to her husband. She suffers and so does her family. The emotional tone of their family life becomes dull, apathetic, inconsistent and irritable. A mother's fatigue permeates family life in a thousand small ways.[2]

[1] Marion Hilliard, *Women and Fatigue* (London: Pan, 1960), p. 13.
[2] Ibid., p. 91.

What I have said does not suggest that I think women should not go back to work. But I think that any woman should consider very carefully her physical resources before she does take a job. It is interesting to note that doctors are now discovering that the symptoms of fatigue and apathy which they used to call "housewife syndrome" are now cropping up so often in working women that the same symptoms are now being called "working-wife syndrome." The fact is that women who have borne the strain of bearing children and who are continuing to carry the strain of giving themselves to a growing family are living with a great deal of stress. They are highly subject to fatigue. Going out to work intensifies stress, and a woman who is considering doing so needs to ask herself: *How much stress can I take?*

Another question we need to ask ourselves is: *At what point do my children not need me at home?* As long as there are children in the home, there are good reasons for the mother to be there too. Betty is a good friend of mine, an efficient and effective public health nurse. She took the job when her only child started school last fall. Not long ago, we visited in my study. She was so upset she smoked four cigarettes over her cup of coffee. "Dianne's sick," she explained, "and here I am looking after other people's problems. I just want to be home with her—sometimes I wish I had never gone back to work." Other working mothers have told me the same thing. "It's just fine when all the kids are OK, but then there are the days when some of them are sick or are having problems."

I know how it feels. During one of my short jaunts out to work, Cammie-Lou, then four years old, became very ill. The anguish and anxiety with which I phoned our competent baby-sitter to ask, "How's Cammie now?" were almost unbearable. And so, as I consider my own career and watch my little ones entering school one after another, I wonder: when could I afford to be out of the home?

I can't help but reflect on the times my mother was home when I was sick. There was the time when all four of us had the mumps, in turn. And Mother was there. I remember "quarantines" as being happy, together times. They were opportunities that Mother bought up to read good books to us, talk with us, tenderly care for her four nestlings. What kinds of times would those have been without Mother? Or later, there were the times when, as menstruation set on fiercely, I would come home cramped and wretched; and Mother would be there to give me a cup of hot tea or lemonade and tuck me into bed—and tell me that being a woman was worth it all. I'm not sure that I would want my daughters to go through those times alone.

Yet another question that needs to be faced: *How much of myself do I have to give a job while I am still concerned with a growing family?* I am an all-or-nothing type myself. How much frustration do women induce in themselves by attempting to work competitively in their professions and still save something of themselves for their families? Some women are obviously more able to do this than are others. We all know working women who seem to keep their homes happy, their kids well looked after, and their husband satisfied. Most of us have come across the other kind of working wife too: bedraggled, frustrated, fatigued—with family to match.

There are other questions to ponder: *What will become of my prayer time? Will I be able to carry on any Christian service? Any ministry in the church? Any work of loving and caring for people in my community?* I must have a settled conviction in my heart that going back to work is the ministry the Lord intends for me, before abandoning some of the other ministries He may have entrusted to me as a mother in the home. God knows us, and He knows our

171

needs. If we are "willing and obedient," He will lead us into the most satisfying kind of life. For some women, that may be to stay home. For others, it may be to reenter a career. In His will, it will be best for us and for all who are involved with us.

As you know by now, I have little patience with the over-glamorized picture of the workaday world which is being presented to women. Nor can I see that going back to work is in any essential way a "liberation" unless it is the best choice for the woman and those who need her.

Consider this: if you have your family when you are fairly young, and then allow time for them to grow up—supposing you take twenty years of your life and devote those years to developing your home and your children—you will still have twenty years left in which to pursue your career. Now I don't know about you. But when I really think that over, I realize that twenty years is probably as long as I would really want to teach school anyhow. Or go to work in an office. Or practice law. Twenty years should be long enough for me to do all of the interesting things in my profession that I might care to do.

One of the plans which I find most attractive is for a woman to use some of the family's later growing-up years to prepare for career years ahead. When I taught high school, I was impressed by one of my colleagues—a sharp, alert woman of about forty-five. She was teaching for her first year. Her children were in university or the last years of high school in the same city where she taught, and she had spent the previous six years going to university herself. She entered the profession with a master's degree. And since she combined talent with excellent preparation, after just two years of teaching she became an art consultant for the school system.

Of course, the decision to study requires a reordering of life almost as great as the decision to go back to work. But programs of study are more flexible than hours of work; many more hours can be spent at home. The woman who lives in a university or college city has every advantage. But any woman who really wants to study can organize to include an evening course from an extension service, or enroll in a correspondence program. It is important before embarking on any sort of study program to consult employment services and guidance personnel to be sure that you are heading in the right direction to reach your particular job goal. The bitter frustration of finding that time has been spent and money wasted on courses which are dead end is one which many women have experienced. Play it safe: decide what your long-range goal is, and then with the help of guidance personnel from a training school, college, university, or manpower center, draw up a program to meet the requirements. It is probably well to remember that courses offered by government agencies are usually both less expensive and more profitable than courses offered by private institutions. Before making a deposit on a commercial home-study course in interior design, for example, I would check to see if a comparable course were available through the public school adult education program, or the college extension program to which I might have access. And I would check with an employment agency to see if (1) the course would provide recognized credentials, and (2) jobs in that field are available within my living area.

Organizing housework around study or work is challenging. Older children should, of course, do their share. But the mother will still be the basic homemaker. The condition and atmosphere of the home will continue to depend upon her ability to get the necessary things done, and leave the unnecessary things undone. One woman with whom I worked maintained a large and beautiful home, a reasonable schedule of entertaining, and a high school family—with the help of a once-a-week cleaning lady and three hours of work each Saturday morning from each of her teenagers. "The children owe that to me," she explained. "I give them specific jobs for that time. In return, I see that they have weekly allowances for bus fares and lunch." She made it clear that she did not pay her children for their work; it was an exchange arrangement in which they all contributed what they were able—she, money; they, time and labor.

Another working woman told me, "I take the family out to dinner at least once a week. That's the sort of thing which takes the pressure out of working." The wife who studies may have to just cope with her work load as best she can; the working wife needs to realize that some of her earnings should be used to lighten the tasks—perhaps buying good automatic appliances, hiring some housekeeping help, or taking the family out for meals.

Of course, widowhood, a husband's disability, or divorce might hasten this transition from housewife back to career woman for some. Then the choices will be less open, the contemplation less leisurely. The woman who becomes, of necessity, the wage-earner for her family can count on God for strength and grace for the adjustments which such a sudden reentry entails. I talked with such a woman a few weeks ago. Her entry into the labor force was caused by her husband's going blind. "I had always been a mother in the home," Dorothy said, "and then suddenly there I was. No training—not even high school. No experience but farm work. And I had to find a way to support us all." Dorothy went back to school and took an adult upgrading program to procure a high school diploma before looking for work. Ben and their two daughters kept the housework done and the meals made. Surviving became a team affair. Now Dorothy is working in a cabinet-making factory. The frequent raises she has been given since starting work a few months ago show that her employer recognizes the quality of her work. And better yet, she noticed a job at the factory that Ben could handle without eyesight—and now they go to work together every morning.

Another friend of mine had her life-style suddenly altered when her husband, a bank manager, died of a heart attack. A woman who had been raised in a large city, Mary found herself widowed in a small town. Her work experience was in stenography, and steno jobs are not plenteous in a little town. But Mary's youngest daughter was still in elementary school, and Mary knew that if she moved to a city to find work, her girl would become a "latchkey kid." So Mary stayed where she was. "Living costs out here are so much lower," she explained, "that I can stay at home, take a boarder, and make ends meet." Mary's story, like Dorothy's, has a happy ending: not long ago, the one good stenographic job in town came up—and Mary got it. Now she is school secretary—working the same hours that her daughter goes to school—a perfect arrangement for them both.

Sometimes a woman has to go to work, as in the cases we have just discussed. But often the financial "needs" which send mothers to work prematurely are little more than a taste for luxury. We have reached a standard of living in our society which is hard to support on one salary—even a generous one. Two salaries are needed to swing the huge house mortgages, two cars, and swimming pools which even average people have come to regard as something they are entitled to have. But the mother who does stay home can economize in many ways: less expensive food preparation since fewer convenience foods are needed, a small garden grown and harvested, children's clothing sewn instead of bought. Even the financial pressure to go back to work can, in most cases, be effectively resisted by the woman who feels that it is best to stay at home. My mother was one of those women. "When you kids were growing up, we could have used the extra money I could have earned," she said. "But I decided to stay home, although lots of my friends were tak-

175

ing jobs. And I have never been sorry." Perhaps her life pattern is one for a generation gone by, or perhaps it is one which we should cherish as an open option for those of us who are wives and mothers.

There are, however, women who truly need to work. Their careers are important to their having an identity. But there are others for whom the greatest satisfaction is simply in staying home—even after the children are grown. Any woman is certainly entitled to quiet years in her own home if that is what her heart desires. Indeed, before simply assuming that she will use the years from age forty to sixty-five for wage-earning, a woman needs to give prayerful consideration to all of the factors that have been mentioned—and others which enter her own circumstance.

Going back to work necessitates a realignment of family finance. And as at every other point of major adjustment in a marriage, love and tact will be necessary. Many husbands still feel threatened by their wives' desire to go back to work. They need to be reassured that they are loved as persons, not merely as breadwinners. Other men fear that wives will use their own earnings as a route to independence. Perhaps it should be said that the money a woman earns is no more her own in any final or ultimate way than the money her husband earns is his own. It will be necessary for her to share as deeply and as freely as he must. Quite likely she will be responsible for paying for any replacement of her own services in the home, and for her own clothing and personal needs as well. Husband and wife may share rent, utilities, and food costs; or the husband may continue to care for those items while she takes over purchasing clothing for the children. On the other hand, a couple may decide to use one of their salaries for savings, investment, or specific capital purchases, and continue to live on the one income they have already had. Any of these arrangements—or endless variations on them—may be the right

176

one for a particular pair of people. But whatever arrangement is decided upon, it needs to be arrived at by mutual agreement. There should be as much mutuality about the use of a wife's earnings as there has been about the use of the husband's.

The real keys to a smooth transition from housewife to career woman are (1) a prayerful waiting on the Lord for His leading, (2) deep communication between husband and wife, (3) a continuation within the marriage relationship of the principles of mutual submission, voluntary submission, and love.

19

Ministering Women

IF THE WOMAN'S PLACE is not necessarily just "in the kitchen," is there any place out of bounds? How about a woman in the pulpit? On the church board? How should we view the question of the woman's place in the church?

As in the early chapters of this book, we again find ourselves confronting some pretty difficult passages of Scripture. Let's look at those in the New Testament which directly concern the woman in her ministry within the church.

> But I would have you know, that the head of every man is Christ; and the head of the woman is the man; and the head of Christ is God.... every woman that prayeth or prophesieth with her head uncovered dishonoureth her head: for that is even all one as if she were shaven. For if the woman be not covered, let her also be shorn: but if it be a shame for a woman to be shorn or shaven, let her be covered (1 Corinthians 11:3, 5-6).

> Let your women keep silence in the churches: for it is not permitted unto them to speak; but they are commanded to be under obedience.... And if they will learn any thing, let them ask their husbands at home: for it is a shame for women to speak in the church (1 Corinthians 14:34-35).

178

Let the woman learn in silence with all subjection. But I suffer not a woman to teach, nor to usurp authority over the man, but to be in silence (1 Timothy 2:11-12).

Clearly, such passages are a bit disconcerting to the modern Christian woman. Now, these writings have been handled by some expositors as being culture-specific, and not applicable to the modern church. This line of exegesis says that the women of the Greek culture, which predominated in Corinth, could not have been entrusted with church authority. As wives, they completely lacked any prior training or education to prepare them for such a role of leadership. Or, as ex-courtesans, they had lived lives of such lasciviousness as to render them dangerous in leadership. Those who argue this way suggest that Paul, were he writing today, would have written something very different.

Since I am a feminist at heart, such interpretations are highly attractive. Nonetheless I find myself uncomfortable in dismissing New Testament teaching in such a way. If "all scripture is given by inspiration of God" (2 Timothy 3:16), then it seems to me we must accept that, while speaking in a particular historical and cultural context, Paul was writing the very Word of God concerning the Church and roles within it. Paul does occasionally let us in on his own thoughts as distinct from God's (as in 1 Corinthians 7:6, 12 ff.), but he is always very careful to make this distinction. It is possible that the phrase "I suffer not the woman to teach" can be taken in this light. Paul, himself, did not allow women to teach. This was his policy, and one which he recommended to Timothy—but it was not laid down as an absolute norm for the Church.

However, there is a weight of evidence in the New Testament that in the Church, an institution created by God Himself, the woman's role was to be analagous to her role in the home: a role of volitional submission to authority or-

179

dained of God. The hierarchy is clearly laid out in 1 Corinthians 11: as Christ submits Himself to God the Father, so men are to submit to Christ, and women to men. "Nevertheless," Paul concludes, "neither is the man without the woman, neither the woman without the man, in the Lord. For as the woman is of the man, even so is the man also by the woman; but all things of God" (1 Corinthians 11:11-12). The interdependency of male and female, as "heirs together of the grace of life" (1 Peter 3:7) is not to be forgotten. The principle which is to govern all interpersonal relationships among Christians is still: "Submitting yourselves one to another" (Ephesians 5:21).

However, before we banish women to the church kitchen to make the fellowship lunch, we need to examine other evidence in the New Testament concerning the woman's role within the Church. It is clear that women *did* pray and prophesy; this is stated in the passage concerning women's head coverings (to which we will refer again a little later). Another revealing passage is found in 1 Timothy 2, the latter part of which we have already quoted. Its context is significant. Having outlined how men should go about public prayer, the writer goes on to say:

> I will therefore that men pray every where, lifting up holy hands, without wrath and doubting. In like manner also, that women adorn themselves in modest apparel (1 Timothy 2:8-9).

Quite clearly, women, too, had a part in public prayer. And relative to that part in public worship, women were to dress modestly so that they would not distract from the worship which they shared in. Both this passage and the one in 1 Corinthians concerning head coverings seem to me to have one basic thrust: the woman who does pray or prophesy— that is, the one who has a place of public leadership within the Church—needs to be especially careful in her dress and demeanor to show that she recognizes her place of submission first, to her husband, and also to the men of the Church. This is not based on any doctrine of inferiority, but rather on a revealed order—God's pattern for His Church.

If the home is "the little church," the Church can be seen as "the big family" (and is called that in Ephesians 3:15). When we see it that way, the same three principles we have discussed in the context of the family apply to the Church context: mutual submission of one to another, voluntary submission of the woman to the man, and undergirding and rationalizing all of them—love. God has ordained in the two institutions which best reveal His love for mankind an order which can be ignored only at great risk both to ourselves and to the institutions.

It is clear, however, that women in the New Testament church were free to exercise the gifts given by the Holy Spirit within the assembly. The passage concerning women's silence in the church seems to me to concern women who were rude or disruptive, interrupting the flow of the service with questions, comments, or perhaps even chit-chat. That sort of thing only promoted confusion, and Paul sternly ruled it out of order. However, the four daughters of the evangelist Philip did prophesy (Acts 21:9); Euodias and Syntyche are named by Paul along with a general reference to "those women which laboured with me in the gospel" (Philippians 4:3). Surely they did more than stuff envelopes or pour tea—to be thus credited. Phebe is named as "a servant of the church," and the Christians at Rome were requested to "assist her in whatsoever business she hath need of you" (Romans 16:1-2). My favorite New Testament woman of all is Priscilla who is named alongside her husband, Aquila, in every reference. Together with him, she was a tentmaker (Acts 18:2-3); together with him, she taught the gospel to a powerful young preacher named

Apollos (Acts 18:24-26); together, this couple is referred to by Paul as "my helpers in Christ Jesus" (Romans 16:3). Yes, there were women who exercised ministries within the first-century church.

Because of the teaching concerning God's order for family and Church, the Church does harbor some men with a strong set of "male chauvinist" ideas—men who have not learned to weigh the revelation that in Christ there is "neither male nor female" equally with "I suffer not a woman to teach." Such men, in or out of pulpits, feel called upon to defend male dominance to the point that they overlook or purposely squelch gifted women within the congregation. The Church is accordingly impoverished. This is clearly not what the Lord intended.

A few years ago, I was asked to be the main speaker at a youth conference. The passages concerning a woman exercising a teaching ministry troubled me, and I brought the matter to the Lord in prayer. One evening before the conference, a group of us met in a home to pray; as we shared from the Word and prayed together, the presence of the Holy Spirit became very real. I mentioned the youth conference as a prayer request, and then I realized that what I really needed was a confirmation of my own calling to the teaching ministry. I told my friends about my concerns—and the fears that they were causing. And then, as I knelt, my friends gathered around me and ministered to me in prayer, laying their hands on me and asking God to speak His directions to me.

The experience of those few moments was both unforgettable and almost inexpressible. Like clear oil, the anointing of the Holy Spirit poured into my troubled heart and left me with a beautiful, quiet peace. My fears fell away. I realized that in God's strength I could do the job. But the Lord knew that I needed one thing more. Beyond the experience, wonderful as it was, I needed the confirming witness of "a more sure word of prophecy" (2 Peter 1:19).

As I rose from my knees, praising the Lord, someone in the group commented upon the unusual pouring out of the Holy Spirit upon young people. "Isn't it foretold in Acts?" I asked. I flipped quickly to Acts 2 and began to read aloud:

> And it shall come to pass in the last days, saith God, I will pour out of my Spirit upon all flesh: and your sons and your daughters shall prophesy, and your young men shall see visions, and your old men shall dream dreams: and on my servants—

Here I had to pause to turn the page. What I saw at the top of the next page made me almost shout with joy!

> *and on my handmaidens* I will pour out in those days of my Spirit; *and they shall prophesy* (Acts 2:17-19, itals. added).

I had no more doubts. The Old Testament prophets had seen a day when God's handmaidens would join in the ministry of the Word, and I was living in that great day of grace. God's Spirit utterly liberated me through His Word.

In summarizing my convictions concerning the place of women in the Church, I see then these principles:

1. The attitude of women in the Church, as in the home, is to be that of voluntary submission.

2. Generally speaking, God will give men the positions of final authority in the Church. This forces upon men the responsibility for spiritual leadership and thus strengthens both the home and the Church.

3. The Holy Spirit gives gifts at His own discretion—and He gives gifts to women as well as to men.

183

4. While a woman is not to "usurp authority" or take it on for herself, the Church leadership may well see fit to invite a woman to exercise her spiritual gift within the assembly, and so enrich the whole fellowship of believers.

5. There is no place within the Church for the ministry of a rebellious woman, one who has not learned "active submission" within her own life. The attitude of meekness which is to characterize all believers must certainly characterize the believing woman who ministers in a public way.

6. For the woman who does exercise a spiritual ministry within the Church, matters of dress and deportment are important and should reveal the beauty of the "hidden man of the heart" (1 Peter 3:4) rather than draw attention to the woman herself.

7. The priority of family responsibilities must be maintained. This in itself places limitations on the public ministry of a wife and mother, since she must respect that her first obligation in time and energy is the care of her family.

8. Ministries of a spiritual nature, whether they be inside or outside the Church, need to be undertaken only at the direction of the Lord Jesus Christ. The woman who cannot say no to the eager program planners may soon find herself overextended and ineffective in her ministry.

I have faced two kinds of problems with regard to my role in the Church. I have experienced being thwarted and hindered in any attempt to minister the Word—and the Lord gave me His comfort, "Thou art my servant; I have chosen thee, and not cast thee away" (Isaiah 41:9). And I have experienced becoming terribly overbusy. Now, I have a small note taped to my telephone. It says, simply, NO. That, and my rule of discussing any activities with my husband before accepting them, help to keep my calendar uncluttered and my strength unsapped. Actually, a woman who has one job within the church—a Sunday school class, a role in the women's fellowship, or a committee or board appointment—has probably all the involvement in church ministry that she should have.

For there are other spheres of ministry for her. There are needy friends at work, neighbors who need to know she cares. Many women are finding a warmly rewarding ministry in their homes by means of neighborhood Bible studies. Others have a less verbal kind of ministry which is just as important. There are women who remember to send a card to a sick person, or visit a new mother with a little gift—not because they are on a "Sunshine Committee" but just because the Lord has given them a ministry of caring. And we must not overlook those silent members of the church whose ministry is that of prayer.

Once when Cam and I were having a particularly successful ministry among young people in a large city church, a single girl who was a friend of ours never failed to ask us how the group was going. She was a new Christian—a shy, introverted girl. We kept her up to date on details, but wondered why she should have such a special interest. Then one day, she explained, "I pray every day for you and Cam in your work with the young people." Then we knew why God was blessing.

Because of the emphasis on spoken witness, many women who engage in silent ministries experience discouragement and feelings of inadequacy. One such woman told me, "I just don't speak easily about the things that are deepest. Another said, "I can always think of the right thing to say—after the moment to say it has passed." Still another, who had given of herself in loving service to a young couple and

185

seemed to be finding no opportunity of sharing Christ with them, was particularly depressed. I was thinking of her and praying for her as I read the Bible one day, and a beautiful verse jumped out at me: "For God is not unrighteous to forget your work and labour of love, which ye have shewed toward his name" (Hebrews 6:10). I printed the reference on a card and handed it to her the next Sunday. It is a verse to comfort the hearts of all ministering women.

For women who feel frustrated because their ministry seems to be a silent one, or one that is almost entirely within the home, Paul's description of the body of Christ should be a source of comfort:

> For the body is not one member, but many . . . if the ear shall say, Because I am not the eye, I am not of the body; is it therefore not of the body? If the whole body were an eye, where were the hearing? If the whole were hearing, where were the smelling? But now hath God set the members every one of them in the body, as it hath pleased him (1 Corinthians 12:14-18).

The whole body is not mouth any more than it is all ear!

Whatever transition you are in, whether you find yourself single or married, housewife or career woman, you will know real joy and release in your life when you pour your whole personality out before the Lord as a "reasonable service" (Romans 12:1). He does not ask you to become like someone else. He asks you to bring to Him what you are and let Him use you. If you have gifts of conversation and social ease, He may have one kind of ministry for you. If you have the gift of a loving and caring heart, He will show you how to minister. As our pastor said recently, "Many people speak of Acts 1:8 as a command. But I see it as a promise: "But ye shall receive power, after that the Holy Ghost is come upon you: and ye *shall* be witnesses unto me."

The total Christian witness is made up of each of us letting Christ live through us, control our lives, and show Himself to those around. Our part is just to make ourselves available to Him—not to scramble about looking for a ministry—but to let God place us within the body as He sees fit, using our personalities and abilities, together with His special gifts—all to the end "that God in all things may be glorified through Jesus Christ, to whom be praise and dominion for ever and ever. Amen" (1 Peter 4:11).

Is This All?

> The problem lay buried, unspoken, for many years in the
> minds of American women. It was a strange stirring, a sense
> of dissatisfaction, a yearning that women suffered.... Each
> suburban wife struggled with it alone. As she made the
> beds, shopped for groceries, matched slipcover material, ate
> peanut butter sandwiches with her children, chauffeured
> Cub Scouts and Brownies, lay beside her husband at
> night—she was afraid to ask even of herself the silent ques-
> tion—"Is this all?"[1]

WITH THIS HAUNTING paragraph, Betty Friedan launched
her epochal book, *The Feminine Mystique*. She put her finger on a problem—"The Problem That Has No Name"—as she
calls it. But while her effort to find an answer is commend-
able, none of the remedies she suggests go far enough to answer that deep question of the heart, "Is this all?"

It is the Christian woman who knows the answer to this
silent query of modern women. Her answer is, "No, of
course this isn't all!" Whether you are a housewife locked
into the day-to-day round of chores for others, or whether
you are a single girl sometimes wistful about having a
family of your own, life is not made up of the sum of individual things we do.

[1] Betty Friedan, *The Feminine Mystique*, p. 13.

It is the Christian woman who can say, "I can let my husband pursue his career, I can let my children grow up and go—because they are not the center of my being. God is, and He is unchanging." And it is the Christian single woman who can say, "My life does not disintegrate because some of my dreams do not come true. Jesus Christ is real and near. I can live life as a single person and live it meaningfully—in Him."

The Christian woman does not envy men, nor compete with them for equality. She does not have to. She knows she is equal, in God's sight and in her own. And this self-assurance speaks for itself wherever she goes. Nor does the Christian woman wish to be like man; she has a much higher calling—to become like Jesus Christ as the Holy Spirit teaches her and works out the very life of Christ within her.

Today, among the milling, restless women of our age, the Christian woman can move with poise and assurance. She is what she is—not because of freaky evolutionary quirks, but because God made her that way. She does not fret against the cycles of menstruation, pregnancy, childbirth, menopause—but accepts them as part of God's design.

The woman who keeps her life centered in the person of Jesus Christ, and refreshed through fellowship with Him, is submissive in the home and in the church. But hers is not a groveling submission of barefooted servitude, but rather the glad love offering of submission to the will of God. In that submission she finds peace and joy and confidence, for she recognizes that God's plan as revealed in the Bible does not hamper or stifle her, but sets her free for full personhood.

As she goes about her daily routines, whether of housework or a job—or both, she is aware that this is not all. God's plans for her reach far beyond the pettiness of each day to an eternity where, "in the ages to come [God will] shew the exceeding riches of his grace in his kindness toward us through Christ Jesus" (Ephesians 2:7). Her life has an ex-

189

tra dimension: the spiritual. And a boundless extension: the eternal. She shares the common Christian hope of the resurrection, but ponders, almost mystified, Christ's words: "In the resurrection they neither marry, nor are given in marriage, but are as the angels of God in heaven" (Matthew 22:30). Whatever all that may mean, it does mean that someday male/female distinctions will be done away with, and for eternity she will know total emancipation together with her brothers in Christ.

Meanwhile, she does not feel that she has a bad deal. If she has chosen wisely, she has her life to share with a loving, godly man; if she is a mother, she has something vital to pass on to another generation—a glorious heritage which she has the opportunity to transmit. If she is single, she recognizes the dignity of her calling from God and serves Him without distraction.

No matter what other panaceas are offered to women today in the name of "liberation," we who know the Lord Jesus Christ in a personal and life-changing relationship of faith, know that when our sisters have tried it all: jobs, independence, money, freedom—they will still be whispering in their hearts, "Is this all?" Until they find Christ.

And so, today, the Christian woman has something to say to the sisterhood of women everywhere. She has good news. Important news. She realizes that to be freed from man-centeredness for self-centeredness is no real liberty. Instead, she offers the invitation to others to know the real freedom of Christ-centered living. Knowing His forgiveness brings her peace, and freedom from guilt. Knowing His promise of eternal life to all who will believe, frees her from the bondage of fear. Knowing that her salvation has been accomplished through His death and not by her efforts frees her from the struggle to achieve acceptance on her own. Knowing His love and truth frees her from feelings of inferiority and the need to somehow prove equality.

190

My sisters in Christ, we are the liberated women of this age! Let us share our good news with those around us, for Jesus came "to proclaim release to the captives, and . . . to set free those who are downtrodden" (Luke 4:18, NASB).